What Peopl

"So many people are worried before retirement hits. One of the largest debts most Americans have is their mortgage. How refreshing is it to be able to show a couple a sure-fire way to reduce their mortgage at an accelerated pace without increasing their monthly mortgage payment? The H.E.A.P.™ concept gives my clients 'freedom.'"

Greg White, Achieve Financial Group, LLC

"H.E.A.P.™ explains how any homeowner with home equity and self-discipline can significantly reduce the duration of their mortgage, and by doing so save thousands of dollars in needless interest expense. This book uses repetition and numerous examples so by the end of the book readers will have a clear sense of how the program works."

Richard M. Sazonoff, Sazonoff Insurance Services

"After reading H.E.A.P.™, I was able to design my own personal program that will allow me to pay off my mortgage in 6 1/2 years rather than 24 years. In addition, I'll reduce my interest payments to the bank by almost $92,000!"

Terry Riely, Secure Solutions

"Roccy does a great job of explaining how to pay off your mortgage early. He has a knack for explaining any topic. In the book, Roccy guides you through a maze of facts with a sense of clarity and a firm grasp of the benefits of paying off your home mortgage early."

Stephen A. Harris, KSP Financial

"One of the main goals my clients have is to own their home free and clear, and in my opinion H.E.A.P.™ is the best way to achieve this goal. With H.EA.P.™, you'll be able to catch up your equity position quicker than with any other alternative, not to mention the best part about H.E.A.P.™…the price."

Ken Schrauben, Equity Proshop

The Home Equity Acceleration Plan (H.E.A.P.™)

Published by KS Publications, Inc.
Copyright © 2011 TriArc Advisors, LLC

KS Publications, Inc.
P.O. Box 36
Etiwanda, CA 91739

ISBN-13   978-0-9842308-2-2

Special thanks to Patrick Yore of Brainblaze (www.brainblaze.com) for designing the book cover for The Home Equity Acceleration Plan (H.E.A.P.™).

The Home Equity Acceleration Plan

(H.E.A.P.™)

Roccy DeFrancesco
JD, CWPP™, CAPP™, CMP™

This book is dedicated to everyone who wants
to pay off their home mortgage 5, 10, even 15+ years early
so they can own their home free and clear.

I hope you enjoy reading this book as much as I enjoyed writing it.

Roccy DeFrancesco
JD, CWPP™, CAPP™, CMP™

Table of Contents

The Home Equity Acceleration Plan
H.E.A.P.™

Acknowledgements

Always at the top of my list are my two loving children, Lauren and Mitchell. They are my inspiration.

On the technical side of the book, I have several people to thank as this book covers many different subject matters (mortgages, financial planning, tax, estate planning, insurance, etc.)

In alphabetical order, I'd like to thank the following people for their contributions to this book:

Brian Balow, Marcia DeFrancesco, Roccy DeFrancesco, Sr., Sujith Kumar, Dean Lemon, Shawn Oosterlinck.

A special thank you to John Steinke who was instrumental with his help in the early phases of getting H.E.A.P.™ off the ground.

Finally, a special thanks to Jim Duggan, JD, MBA of Duggan Bertsch, LLC. Mr. Duggan donated his time to create the **H.E.A.P.™ Charitable Foundation**.

Foreword

Would you like to pay off your home mortgage debt 5-10-15+ years early with a plan:

-that does **NOT require you to change your lifestyle**;

-that allows you to **stay in complete control** of the plan; and

-where the **average person will save over $100,000** in mortgage interest with a new loan?

If you are like most readers, your answer will be not only yes, but a resounding YES!

Most people have a handful of days in their lives that they will never forget. I'm not sure what your specific list would look like but it might include:

-the day you got married (I remember that day, because it was the hottest day of the year and the church had no air conditioning).

-the day your children were born (I have two and I will never forget those days and the experience).

-while not pleasant days, you may remember the day we initially went to war the first time in Iraq (I was taking final exams in college); or 9-11 when, incredibly and tragically, planes were flown into the twin towers in NY (I was playing golf with my dad, Roccy, Sr. at that time).

-the day the Chicago Cubs won the World Series (forget this one. It has not happened yet during my life and probably never will).

How about the following day?

The day you made your last mortgage payment on your personal residence (I paid off the mortgage on my home at the age of 34, and I'll never forget the feeling of knowing I would not have to allocate money to mortgage payments).

Side note:

After researching whether it is more economically beneficial to pay off the debt on a personal residence or having the most possible debt on it while using all available money to build wealth elsewhere, I promptly sold my house with no debt on it and built a new one with significant debt.

If you are curious why I would do such a thing (since it sounds counterintuitive and does not follow H.E.A.P.™), you should consider reading my book titled **The Home Equity Management Guidebook: How to Achieve Maximum Wealth with Maximum Security**. You can read about the book at www.thehomeequitymanagementguidebook.com.

I also have a short summary in this book (Chapter 6) briefly explaining why you may choose not to aggressively pay off the debt on your home.

If you are like most of the people who purchase this book, you haven't yet reached that memorable day when you made your last mortgage payment. In fact, most people who purchase this book have as one of their highest priorities the goal of paying off their home mortgage.

WHAT LIES AHEAD?

This book is laid out in a simple and easy-to-follow manner. First I'm going to explain a little about mortgages in general. Learning these basics will help you better understand the remaining parts of the book (including how H.E.A.P.™ works).

I will then explain how the old-school mortgage acceleration plans work (Rounding-Up, Applying the Bonus, and Bi-Weekly Plans).

Then the majority of this book will discuss how H.E.A.P.™ works and its multiple uses to help you reduce debt, give you more control of your financial situation, and pay off your mortgage significantly quicker than the old-school mortgage acceleration plans.

Finally, and not an insignificant portion of this book, I will tell you in Chapter 5 about what I call the "Bad" and the "Ugly" mortgage acceleration plans in the marketplace that you'll want to stay way from. When you learn how the "Bad" and "Ugly" acceleration plans are sold, it will outrage you I'm sure.

HOW CAN YOU RECEIVE HELP WITH H.E.A.P.™?

One question you may have after reading this book is how can you use H.E.A.P.™ to potentially pay off your mortgage 5-10-15+ years early saving tens of thousands of dollars in mortgage interest over the life of your loan.

The bad news is that I can't tell you in this book the specifics of how many years you can knock off of your mortgage and how much in interest you personally could save by using H.E.A.P.™

If you know a local H.E.A.P.™ advisor, I strongly recommend you contact him/her so he/she can run specific numbers to determine how quickly you can pay off your mortgage and how many tens of thousands of dollars in mortgage interest you will save using the plan.

The good news is that, if you do not know a local H.E.A.P.™ advisor, you can go to http://www.HEAPlan.com and fill out a request for information/proposal form; and you will be forwarded the contact information of a local advisor who can help you with H.E.A.P.™

An advisor who is familiar with H.E.A.P.™ and has the needed software to properly budget your plan can usually do so in very short order. You will receive from your local advisor a three-page printout that will tell you specifically how many years H.E.A.P.™ will knock off your mortgage and how many thousands (and for some hundreds of thousands) of dollars in interest you will save.

I can tell you from talking with literally hundreds of interested clients that the excitement/anticipation of receiving a H.E.A.P.™ proposal is significant (sort of like waiting for a Christmas gift you know is coming).

I highly recommend that you do not hesitate to fill out the form online to start the process of paying down your mortgage sooner rather than later by using H.E.A.P.™

And now without further ado, let's move onto the rest of the book where you will learn about the very powerful Home Equity Acceleration Plan (H.E.A.P.™).

The H.E.A.P.™ Charitable Foundation
www.HEAPlan.org

It dawned on me while writing this book that this country is truly having a mortgage and overall financial crisis.

There are tens of thousands of Americans who are struggling to pay their monthly mortgage payment. I do not want to go into all of the reasons why people can't pay their mortgage; however, I will tell you that I live in the state of Michigan, which has been devastated by the downturn in the auto industry.

There are thousands of people just in the state of Michigan who have lost their jobs through no fault of their own and many are in dire financial situations.

What happens when you lose your job and can't find another one for weeks/months/years? You end up living on your savings, if you have any.

What happens when you run out of money from your saving(s) account(s)? That's when the rubber really hits the road. Some people will live on credit cards for awhile; but, ultimately, the money will run out and bills will not be paid.

What is the largest monthly bill for most people? Their home mortgage.

What's one of the most important bills to pay? The home mortgage.

Why? Because, ultimately, if you do not pay your mortgage on a consistent basis, you will lose your home. I've never been in a situation where I could potentially lose my home due to financial circumstances, but I can imagine it is one of worst and most fearful feelings in the world.

PUT YOUR MONEY WHERE YOUR MOUTH IS

If you read the Foreword to this book, you know that one of the reasons I created H.E.A.P.™ was due to my disdain for the **$3,500** "Bad" mortgage acceleration program that is currently in the marketplace. My goal in creating H.E.A.P.™ was to put forth the only "client-friendly" mortgage acceleration plan in the marketplace.

My goal with this book is to tell you the truth about how mortgage acceleration plans work so you can decide for yourself which one is best for you.

When you read Chapter 5, you may come away with the impression that I have some "do-right" gene. I don't necessarily think that's the case, but I fully believe that some people are programmed from their childhood/upbringing and that there are some people in this world who do not mind speaking out when they see a need.

While many of you do not know me yet, I can tell you that I am very outspoken in the professional (financial, insurance, mortgage, accounting, and legal) fields that I work in. I routinely call people out from these fields in my nationally published newsletters when I think they are doing something wrong and not in their client's best interest. Doing so doesn't make me any better than anyone else; it just makes me a bit different since few people have a business model that allows them not to worry about upsetting the very people they look to in order to make a living.

Recently I took my outspokenness to a new level when I published my new book **Bad Advisors: How to Identify Them; How to Avoid Them** (**www.badadvisors.com**). My Bad Advisors book is a dirty little secrets book that will blow the minds of most readers. If you ever wondered if your current advisors are any good or if you would like to make sure you can determine if a future advisor is any good, I strongly recommend you obtain a copy of the book (and yes, in the book I discuss mortgage acceleration plans and specifically comment on the $3,500 program).

I try very hard to "walk the walk and talk the talk" with my advice to advisors and to their clients. My motto and that of those who become certified advisors through The Wealth Preservation Institute (**www.thewpi.org**) is to **always do what is in the client's best interest no matter how that affects your compensation**.

This motto makes complete sense to me due to the fact that, if you do what's right for your clients (no matter what industry you are in), you will be in business a long time, create a loyal client following, and usually receive many referrals from your clients.

Literally a few days before this book was supposed to be printed, I was driving down the road and came up with what I thought was a pretty good idea. Why not take a book which is about helping many people seeking to do the right thing for themselves (which is to pay off mortgage debt as quickly as possible), and do the right thing by donating ALL of the proceeds from the sale of this book to homeowners who need it?

The moment the thought came into my head I knew it was the right thing to do; and, so I added this short summary of how I plan on using H.E.A.P.™ to help everyday Americans pay their mortgage payment when they are in financial distress.

HOW WILL THE H.E.A.P.™ CHARITABLE FOUNDATION WORK?

I plan on making this extremely simple for me and, in turn, for you to understand.

I am charging $24.95 for my book plus shipping (if you have to pay shipping).

I also have H.E.A.P.™ software advisors can purchase to illustrate this powerful concept to their clients.

I can also sell software directly to consumers who want to use it to help them maximize the benefits of using H.E.A.P.™

I charge advisors a first year fee of $500 to use the software and then $150 a year to keep access to it. I charge consumers who want to use the software $200 as a one-time fee for a lifetime license (to learn more about the software, please go to **www.heaplan.com**).

I then take ALL the money I make from the sale of the book and the software and donate it a 501(c) charitable entity called the H.E.A.P.™ Charitable Foundation. That Foundation will then use the donated money to help homeowners in need on a local level.

The H.E.A.P.™ Charitable Foundation will give money directly to homeowners in need and will also give money to other local charities that want to be involved. Local charities may include churches, community foundations, etc.

I have no idea how many books will sell or how many licenses to the software I will sell, but I do believe this is one of the most important books written about mortgages due to the fact that, if the advice is followed, the positive financial outcome for readers will literally be life changing. If that proves to be the case, I imagine one way or another I will be able to donate a decent amount of money to the non-profit every year.

How will I determine which charities will receive money? That's fairly simple. If book sales come from my own marketing, I will distribute those proceeds first locally in my community directly from the H.E.A.P.™ Charitable Foundation. I know my local community has many homeowners in need and who could use the money.

It is my belief and hope that this book will become sort of a cult hit and that various people from around the country will want to get the book out to people they know in their local communities. If someone (maybe such as you) picks up the ball to market this book in a local community, the H.E.A.P.™ Charitable Foundation will donate the money to another 501(c) charity in that local area.

The simplest example of this would be a church or a series of churches in a local community.

Additionally, various Associations or Societies (local and national) may choose to get the book out to their members. If that happens, the H.E.A.P.™ Charitable Foundation will work with these entities to distribute money to charities that the Associations or Societies support.

LET'S TAKE THE GIVING-UP A NOTCH

Because most of my clients these days are the advisors who take my certification courses through the Wealth Preservation Institute, I have had and will have many of these advisors buy the H.E.A.P.™ software I created to help them properly illustrate the power of this topic to their clients.

I will be asking them to donate some portion of the money they make because of their use of H.E.A.P.™ to this charitable cause.

For example, a mortgage broker might start advertising to help clients with H.E.A.P.™ in a local marketplace. If the mortgage broker ends up creating a relationship with a client because of H.E.A.P.™ and at some point in the future helps that client with a mortgage, the advisor might make anywhere from $500 - $2,500+ on the mortgage sale.

I will be formally asking all advisors who become involved in H.E.A.P.™ to donate X amount of their profits to the H.E.A.P.™ Charitable Foundation which will finally help needy homeowners who cannot pay their mortgages. **I can't mandate this**, but I will be asking for them to participate.

I'd like to give you projections for how much money can be raised due to the efforts of the advisors who are and will be helping their clients with H.E.A.P.™, but I really don't know what that might be. I hope to raise tens of thousands of dollars each year with this effort, and I hope to keep it going for years to come (even when our economy finally turns around).

HOW DO YOU FIND OUT MORE ABOUT THE H.E.A.P.™ CHARITABLE CAUSE?

You can learn more about the H.E.A.P.™ charitable cause by going to www.HEAPlan.org.

I welcome input and help from any and all who would like to become involved.

If you would like to help introduce this book to a church, association, or other entity in your local community, please e-mail info@HEAPlan.com. I will get on the phone with you within a few days to figure out the best way to help you get the book out and track the sales so the profits from book sales can come back to your community.

A SPECIAL THANKS

I like to formally thank Jim Duggan, JD, MBA, of the Duggan Bertsch, LLC (www.dugganbertsch.com). Jim is a personal friend of mine who is a terrific attorney with a big heart.

Jim and his law firm have stepped up their giving by donating their time to create and help manage the H.E.A.P.™ Charitable Foundation at no cost to me and with no reimbursement agreement from the Foundation.

SUMMARY ON CHARITABLE CAUSE

Again, when I created H.E.A.P.™ and wrote this book, I had no intention to take up the charge of a charitable cause. However, after coming up with the idea, it took me virtually no time to determine that giving ALL of the profits from the sale of this book as well as any software sales to a charity is an idea that I could fully embrace.

I hope you fully enjoy the rest of the book you are about to read, and I am confident that you will learn how to pay off your own mortgage years earlier thereby saving you tens of thousands of dollars. That's good for you, and there is nothing wrong with that. However, keep in mind that you can help others who are in need by spreading the word about this book. I, and the people who are involved in this effort, would very much appreciate your help.

Chapter 1
My Introduction to
Mortgage Acceleration Plans

Mortgage acceleration plans seem to be getting a lot of traction these days.

Why?

I suppose it makes a lot of sense with the mortgage industry in a bit of an upheaval.

When home mortgage lending rates were low in 2006 and prior, it seemed that many people were **removing** equity from their homes to build wealth or to simply spend it. Paying off a home mortgage was **not** a high priority.

In 2007, the mortgage industry went into a real tail spin. Many consumers were sold short-term Adjustable Rate Mortgages (ARM) that refinanced into much higher interest rate loans when the ARM came due. Most of these loans accelerated the payments to pay off the mortgage in the original term which, in addition to the higher interest rate, significantly increased the required monthly payments.

Because of the media focus continues in 2011 to be on mortgages and consumer debt and because consumers themselves are feeling the pinch of a tough economy, the entire country seems ready to learn about mortgage acceleration plans and ways to get rid of debt (so people can take back some control of their lives).

WHEN DID I LEARN ABOUT MORTGAGE ACCELERATION PLANS?

I learned about mortgage acceleration plans back in 2005 when visiting an advisor who had recently taken the Certified Wealth Preservation Planner (CWPP™) course (www.thewpi.org/cwpp) in Olympia, Washington.

This advisor said that he ran across some "**new**" way to pay off a home mortgage early and that I had to look at it.

I basically said: What could possibly be new in the area of paying off a mortgage quicker? I figured he was talking about bi-weekly payment plans.

Because the advisor persisted, I sat down to listen to him tell me how the plan works; and after a few minutes, I had a good feel for the power of a true Home Equity Acceleration Plan.

Even though I understood the value of this "new" and unique process by which you can pay down a mortgage 5-10-15+ years sooner where the interest savings could easily be in excess of $100,000, it really didn't interest me due to the fact that my core business is to educate CPAs, attorneys, financial planners, insurance agents, and mortgage brokers about advanced planning for the wealthy (www.thewpi.org).

TWO YEARS GO BY

Two years after the advisor in Washington showed me how I could have cut the life of a mortgage by 15+ years, I received a call from an advisor who wanted me to review and market....you guessed it, a "new" kind of mortgage acceleration program.

The person who called me, and who shall go nameless, told me how he came from a company called **Primerica** and how he recently became part of a new company that was created to sell a "new" and "magical" mortgage acceleration plan.

Since I'm basically in the financial services business, I'm very familiar with Primerica. The reputation of Primerica is that of a quasi multi-level marketing (MLM) company where many of the people making the most money are those who recruit new advisors to join up and sell Primerica products (which is odd as you would think the people actually selling the products would make the most money).

This person went on for about an hour telling me how, with the Primerica model, his mortgage acceleration plan would sweep the nation. He indicated that the fee for a client to implement this "new" mortgage acceleration plan was **$3,500**.

That certainly got my attention, and he knew it. The person I was talking with knew that I had over 200,000 financial planners in my e-mail database who receive my weekly educational newsletter, and he told me I could make a fortune "recruiting" those agents to sell this "new" mortgage acceleration plan.

When it was my turn to speak, I explained to this person that I was quite familiar with this "new" mortgage acceleration plan as it was fully explained to me by an advisor in Washington State several years earlier (and in much less than an hour).

I told this person that I had no doubt that his quasi-MLM platform would help spread this "new" program due to the **greed of the advisors** who will go out and recruit other advisors and non-advisors to sell the program.

I told him I thought it was an **outrage** to charge clients **$3,500** for their program when all clients really need to do is sit down with an advisor who understands the subject and can help them implement the plan in very short order without "magic" software.

I figured a fee of $495 or so was reasonable to explain and help a client set up this new kind of mortgage acceleration plan but certainly not **$3,500**. I will explain in much greater detail the problems with the sales pitch of the **$3,500** program in Chapter 5 where I discuss Mortgage Acceleration Plans to Stay Away From.

EQUITY HARVESTING

While I didn't need additional motivation to create H.E.A.P.™, I found some in the national craze that was taking hold in the life insurance and financial services field. That craze—which continues today—is the concept of Equity Harvesting.

Equity Harvesting is a fancy term for removing as much equity from your home as possible so you can reposition that equity into a wealth-building tool where money will grow tax-fee and can be removed tax-free in retirement.

Equity Harvesting is basically the opposite of H.E.A.P.™ which helps you rid yourself of debt, not pile it on in an effort to grow more wealth elsewhere.

The theory behind Equity Harvesting is that it is NOT a good financial move to aggressively pay down debt on your home. That can be true for some (or even many) people as you will read in an abbreviated chapter in this book (Chapter 6).

At approximately the same time I received the phone call from one of the creators of the **$3,500** quasi-MLM mortgage acceleration plan, I had been getting inundated with calls from advisors asking me my opinion of two books in the marketplace that discuss the concept of Equity Harvesting.

As I stated, I have over 200,000 advisors who receive my weekly educational e-newsletter, and many of them look to me for opinions on books, sales concepts, case design, etc.

Those books on Equity Harvesting that advisors were referring to are: <u>Missed Fortune 101</u> and <u>Stop Sitting on Your Assets</u>. You can read about both at <u>http://www.www-MissedFortune101.com</u> and <u>http://www.www-StopSittingOnYourSssets.com</u> (the second www in the address stands for **W**hat's **W**rong **W**ith).

To make a long story short, I read both books prior to being inundated with calls about them; and, I came to the conclusion that both books were two of the **worst books I have ever read** from a "**technical**" standpoint.

If you are the kind of person who reads a book on financial issues and then checks the numbers for yourself with Excel spreadsheets and other tools, then you can relate to my way of thinking.

I broke both books down bit by bit, and I came to the conclusion that any advisor selling clients the strategies as explained in either book better have their Errors & Omissions (liability coverage for professionals) paid up.

Why? Because, sooner or later when the clients figure out that the math used to make the sale of an Equity Harvesting plan was "fuzzy" and/or "defective," lawsuits will start flying (which is actually happening to many advisors in the financial services field today).

One thing that struck me as odd with both books is that they basically (not in these specific words) **called readers stupid** if they did not take the advice of the authors.

What advice?

In general, to remove nearly all of your home's equity so you can reposition it into a wealth-building tool called cash value life insurance (where money can grow tax-free and be removed tax-free in retirement).

I don't think authors should essentially call their readers stupid, especially when it comes to a very emotional and touchy subject like home mortgage debt. As I stated earlier, we as an American culture, believe that one of the greatest days of our lives is the day we pay off our mortgage.

Therefore, I do not call you stupid if you do not remove equity from your house to build wealth. In fact, as you will read in the mini-chapter on Equity Harvesting in this book, I state that even if you understand the positives of Equity Harvesting and how it can help you build "Maximum Wealth with Maximum Security," if it helps you to sleep at night, I strongly advocate that you use H.E.A.P.™ and pay off your home mortgage as soon as possible.

Money is not everything in life and paying down a home mortgage in the quickest manner possible using H.E.A.P.™ is going to fit the personality of many more readers than will taking $10,000-$250,000+ in more debt out on a home in order to build more wealth through Equity Harvesting. Paying down debt quickly and not giving money to a bank makes you feel good, and being debt free gives you options in life you would not otherwise have.

Getting to know my personality as is the case with those who read my books, you may be able to guess what I decided to do after receiving many calls from advisors telling me how wonderful the books on Equity Harvesting that use "fuzzy" math are.

Right. I decided to write my own book so the general public and advisors could learn the proper use of Equity Harvesting. My new book, which came out just prior to this H.E.A.P.™ book, is called **The Home Equity Management Guidebook: How to Achieve Maximum Wealth with Maximum**

Security.   You   can   read   about   at www.thehomeequitymanagementguidebook.com.

My point with this story, besides to put in a shameless plug for my other book, is to help you understand my motivation for moving into the mortgage space.

I believe there is a great need for education of the consumer and the advisors who give them advice. I believe with my <u>Home Equity Management Guidebook</u> and with the H.E.A.P.™ program, I have done my best to provide compliant and honest education to help you make sure you are not taken advantage of by advisors giving bad advice.

THE CREATION OF H.E.A.P.™

After being inundated with calls about defective Equity Harvesting books and after my phone call with the person pitching me this **$3,500** quasi-MLM mortgage acceleration plan, I made what has now become one of those "life-altering decisions." I decided that I needed to not only educate the general public and advisors on mortgage acceleration plans through a new book, but I also needed to create a systematic program that could be used to illustrate and setup such a plan.

That's when I decided to create a mortgage acceleration plan that could be offered to advisors through what is now known as the **Home Equity Acceleration Plan** (H.E.A.P.™).

I wanted to create a program that was not currently available in the market and one that had the **client's, not the advisor's, best interest in mind**.

I wanted to create a program where the advisor could NOT charge more than $500 to help a client set up and implement a plan. As I stated previously, I allow advisors to buy access to the H.E.A.P.™ software and illustration system for a small fee. Then they are allowed to charge up to but <u>not to exceed</u> $500 for their advice to help a client understand the power of H.E.A.P.™, figure their budget, and set up the plan.

WHY ME?

So there's my story—how someone like me, who had no interest in the mortgage field, ended up writing two books on home equity management and spent time and money to create H.E.A.P.™ (a software/illustration system to help people pay off their mortgage years early with a plan that they are in complete control of and one that doesn't require them to change their lifestyle).

Not many advisors in the country have the privilege to right a wrong or stop an injustice that is happening to the American public. Not many advisors can choose to shut their lives down for several months while devoting themselves to writing a book to educate the public or create software to help advisors provide better advice.

But my business model affords me just that opportunity. My model is to help the American public by providing the best education and tools possible to their trusted financial, tax, legal, accounting, insurance, and mortgage advisors through the Wealth Preservation Institute (www.thewpi.org).

Since I don't have to sell any products, my business model allows me to spend 1-2-3-6+ months rolling out new educational courses to help advisors provide the best advice to their clients. It also allowed me to create my two books on home equity management, as well as an illustration system/calculator to support H.E.A.P.™ . So that's how this book ended up in your hands.

It is my hope that you will enjoy reading this book as much as I enjoyed writing it. Also, if you have any questions, please feel free to go to www.HEAPlan.com and contact me from there.

Oh, one last thing….

WHY WON'T YOUR ADVISORS KNOW MANY OF THE TOPICS COVERED IN THIS BOOK?

(Or, If They Know the Topics, Why They Learned Them from Biased Sources)

Let's start with a different question. Has your CPA/EA/accountant, financial planner, insurance agent, mortgage broker, real estate agent, or attorney ever sat you down to discuss proper home equity management?

For 95+% of the readers the answer will be NO. For those who have, the advisor probably sat you down to try and sell you Equity Harvesting based off a defective sales book or a **$3,500** equity acceleration plan.

So, the question of why don't most advisors know many of the topics covered in this book is one I hear commonly when educating clients on H.E.A.P.™. The answer: Because there is no formal educational body in the country that educates on it.

If you like what you read in this book and think your local advisors can benefit by learning about it, please feel free to send them to www.thewpi.org where they can learn more about becoming a certified advisor.

Chapter 2
Mortgage Basics

INTRODUCTION

You have to walk before you run; and in this context, that means you need to know the basics about mortgages in order to fully understand the principals discussed in this book.

This chapter, frankly, is a little more than you need; but I prefer to give you more information rather than less, because understanding mortgages will help you not only with H.E.A.P.™ but will also help you the next time you get a mortgage.

Most readers, at one time or another, have researched the various options for traditional home mortgages. Isn't it true that most people know the basics about 30-year and 15-year amortization mortgages sold by local banks or mortgage brokers?

Isn't it true that most people have heard of 1-, 3-, and 5-year adjustable rate mortgage (ARM) programs?

Isn't it true that most people have heard of interest-only loans?

While not everyone is familiar with loans that have the interest pegged to the **London Inter Bank Offering Rates** (LIBOR), many are.

Won't most readers know how to pay off their mortgage in X years instead of 30 years on a 30-year amortization mortgage? Sure—simply make an extra payment each year, and you turn a 30-year mortgage into a 24-year mortgage (more or less).

If this is all true, why do I feel the need to teach you about mortgages?

Because there are still many things you probably don't know—things you need to know in order to protect yourself from mortgage professionals who do not work from a "client-first" ethic and to help you understand how H.E.A.P.™ can work to help you pay off your mortgage 5-10-15+ years early.

The first part of this chapter will deal with what I'll call MICRO information on home loans, and the second part of this chapter will deal with what I'll call MACRO information.

By reading the MICRO information in the early part of this chapter, you will learn the most important information for understanding how H.E.A.P.™ works and how it can be used to pay down your mortgage 5-10-15+ years earlier.

The MACRO information is very important as well, empowering you with "inside info" on mortgages—which can save you money and heartache.

MIRCO INFORMATION ON MORTGAGES

THE BASICS OF MORTGAGE INTEREST

Since the core information in this book is about reducing mortgage debt, it is most important that you first understand how a mortgage is put together.

What is a residential home loan?

Generally speaking, it's when a lender agrees contractually to lend money to a borrower using a home as collateral for a specific period of time at a specific interest rate.

Based upon the terms, a monthly payment is established so that the loan will be completely paid off at the end of the term of the loan. If the interest rate chosen is an adjustable rate, the monthly payment may change periodically because it is recalculated when the interest rate changes.

Each loan payment has a **principal** and **interest** component to it. As most people who have a mortgage know (usually to their disdain) in the early years of paying back a loan, nearly the entirety of each payment is allocated to mortgage interest. It isn't until the last few years that the majority of each payment is applied to pay down the principal balance.

Therefore, the lender makes the majority of its income from a home loan in the early years and not much toward the end of the lending term.

MORTGAGE PAYMENTS ARE MADE IN ARREARS

It is also important to understand the concept that mortgage payments are made in "arrears." What does that mean? It means that when you make a mortgage payment you are making it to pay for **last month's** interest.

Why is this important? Because mortgage acceleration plans are typically designed to accelerate your payments (even if only by a day, 15 days, or 30 days). **When you pay your mortgage payment or a portion of your payment early, that will lessen the daily interest charged on the loan.**

Because of this fundamental element of mortgage acceleration plans, it is important to keep it in the back of your mind as you are reading through the rest of the book.

MORTGAGE CALCULATIONS

While most people understand the concept of principal and interest as two components of a loan, seeing the actual numbers is a great way to drive home how beneficial H.E.A.P.™ can be when helping you pay off your mortgage early

Let's now look at the math and how mortgage payments are calculated. For the upcoming examples, I am going to use a $200,000 primary mortgage balance with a 30-year amortization (because you are probably most familiar with this commonly used mortgage).

Keep in mind that any amortizing loan (one that pays off completely in a specified period of time) has a principal and interest component.

If a **$200,000** loan has an interest rate of 6.5% for a 30-year fully amortized loan, the monthly payment for the life of the loan would be **$1,264.14**.

The monthly payment must then be broken down into the interest part of the loan and the part that is applied to pay down the principal loan balance.

The interest-only part of the loan would be $1,083.33 in the first month: $200,000 x .065 = $13,000 (annual interest) / 12 (months) = $1,083.33

What most people try not to think about is the fact that in the early years of the loan very little of the loan balance is reduced.

For this example, after the first monthly payment was made, there would be a remaining principal balance of $199,819.19

$1,264.14 (payment) – $1,083.33 (interest charged) = **$180.81** that is applied to paying down the principal loan balance.

$200,000 (original loan balance) – $180.81 (amount of payment that is applied towards principal balance) = 199,819.19 (new balance).

Going into the **second month**, the **interest charges are calculated on the remaining balance**. So the math is:

$199,819.19 (balance) x .065 (interest rate) / 12 (months) = $1,082.35 (interest for 2nd month).

That means the payment of $1,264.14 would pay $181.79 towards the balance (98 cents more than the previous month).

$1,264.14 (payment) – $1,082.35 (interest) = $181.79 (amount of payment applied to the remaining loan balance).

Based on these calculations, you can start to see how over time the balance is slowly reduced in the early years of a mortgage. Since the interest is calculated on the remaining balance, the interest charges reduce over time.

Because the monthly mortgage payment amount remains the same, over time, the amount applied towards interest shrinks, while the amount applied to principal increases.

Take a look at the following real-live amortization schedule for a loan taken out in 2007. The schedule represents the annual amounts paid towards interest and principal. It also shows the remaining balance at the end of each year.

Loan Balance: $200,000; Interest Rate: 6.5%
First Payment: Jan.1, 2007 Monthly Payment: $1,264.14

Year	Total Payment	Interest Due	Applied to Principal	Remaining Balance
2007	$15,169.68	$12,934.23	$2,235.45	$197,764.55
2008	$15,169.68	$12,784.52	$2,385.16	$195,379.39
2009	$15,169.68	$12,624.78	$2,544.90	$192,834.48
2010	$15,169.68	$12,454.34	$2,715.34	$190,119.14
2011	$15,169.68	$12,272.49	$2,897.19	$187,221.95
2012	$15,169.68	$12,078.46	$3,091.22	$184,130.73
2013	$15,169.68	$11,871.43	$3,298.25	$180,832.49
2014	$15,169.68	$11,650.55	$3,519.13	$177,313.35
2015	$15,169.68	$11,414.86	$3,754.82	$173,558.54
2016	$15,169.68	$11,163.40	$4,006.28	$169,552.25
2017	$15,169.68	$10,895.09	$4,274.59	$165,277.66
2018	$15,169.68	$10,608.81	$4,560.87	$160,716.79
2019	$15,169.68	$10,303.36	$4,866.32	$155,850.47
2020	$15,169.68	$9,977.45	$5,192.23	$150,658.24
2021	$15,169.68	$9,629.72	$5,539.96	$145,118.28
2022	$15,169.68	$9,258.70	$5,910.98	$139,207.30
2023	$15,169.68	$8,862.83	$6,306.85	$132,900.45
2024	$15,169.68	$8,440.45	$6,729.23	$126,171.22
2025	$15,169.68	$7,989.78	$7,179.90	$118,991.32
2026	$15,169.68	$7,508.93	$7,660.75	$111,330.57
2027	$15,169.68	$6,995.887	$8,173.81	$103,156.76
2028	$15,169.68	$6,448.46	$8,721.22	$94,435.54
2029	$15,169.68	$5,864.38	$9,305.30	$85,130.24
2030	$15,169.68	$5,241.19	$9,928.49	$75,201.75
2031	$15,169.68	$4,576.26	$10,593.42	$64,608.32
2032	$15,169.68	$3,866.80	$11,302.88	$53,305.44
2033	$15,169.68	$3,109.82	$12,059.86	$41,245.58
2034	$15,169.68	$2,302.15	$12,867.53	$28,378.06
2035	$15,169.68	$1,440.39	$13,729.29	$14,648.77
2036	$15,169.68	$520.91	$14,648.77	$0.00

Wow, I find the previous chart depressing. You probably do too, which is why the idea of paying down a mortgage 5-10-15+ years early with H.E.A.P.™ is so appealing

Let's take a little closer look at the amortization schedule. In the first year, the total monthly payments equal $15,169.68.

$1,264.14 (monthly) x 12 (number of payments) = $15,169.68.

Of the total payments made, **$2,235.45** is applied to pay down the principal loan balance and **$12,934.23** is paid as interest.

Now skip down to year **2017**, which is the **tenth** year of the loan. The same amount of $15,169.68 is paid that year; however, **$4,274.59** is applied to principal and **$10,895.09** towards interest.

Let's take a little test to see if you understand what most think is simple math.

Let's try to calculate how much interest is due in 2018.

Using a simple interest calculation, a "reasonable" estimate of how much interest is due in 2018 can be determined.

$165,277.66 (balance at end of 2017) X .065 (interest rate) = $10,743.05

Is the calculation correct?

Looking back at the chart, the actual interest charges for 2018 are $10,**608**.81, not $10,**743**.05. Why is the actual amount a little less than what we manually calculated? Because the manual calculation was for an **annual amount**.

Remember that the payments are applied **monthly**; each month that a payment is made, the principal balance is slightly reduced; and, therefore, the interest charges are also slightly reduced.

This may seem insignificant to you as I'm going over it, but part of the reason H.E.A.P.™ works to help you pay off your mortgage early revolves around lessening daily interest paid by "**using every available dollar every day**" to pay down mortgage debt. Doing this will lessen the overall interest paid on your loan.

Let's look at each month of the year 2018 and how these payments are applied towards interest and principal.

Date	Interest	Principal	Balance
Jan, 2018	$895.26	$368.88	$164,908.78
Feb, 2018	$893.26	$370.88	$164,537.90
Mar, 2018	$891.25	$372.89	$164,165.01
Apr, 2018	$889.23	$374.91	$163,790.10
May, 2018	$887.20	$376.94	$163,413.16
Jun, 2018	$885.16	$378.98	$163,034.18
Jul, 2018	$883.11	$381.03	$162,653.14
Aug, 2018	$881.04	$383.10	$162,270.05
Sep, 2018	$878.97	$385.17	$161,884.87
Oct, 2018	$876.88	$387.26	$161,497.61
Nov, 2018	$874.78	$389.36	$161,108.26
Dec, 2018	$872.67	$391.47	$160,716.79

The above chart might also get you to think of how little the person in the example has paid down the principal loan balance after making the $1,264.14 payment every month for 12 years.

The person in this example made 144 payments (12 years x 12 payments per year) for a total of $182,036.16. That's a lot of money to have a debt reduction of only $39,283.21.

$200,000 (beginning balance) - $160,716.79 (balance 12/2018) = $39,283.21.

This means that, over the 12-year period, the borrower paid $142,752.95 in interest.

$182,036.16 (total of all payments through 2018) - $39,283.21 (amount applied towards principal) = $142,752.95.

Because most borrowers understand that paying a home mortgage is making a bank a lot of money through interest payments and removing money from their pockets, many are motivated to pay off the debt on their home as early as possible.

Now let's look at the year 2026. This year would represent the 20th year of the 30-year loan. Notice anything special about 2026?

Date	Interest	Principal	Balance
2025	$7,989.78	$7,179.90	$118,991.32
2026	**$7,508.93**	**$7,660.75**	**$111,330.57**
2027	$6,995.87	$8,173.81	$103,156.76

2026 is the first year that the amount applied towards principal is more than the amount paid in interest. And it only took 20 years! Twenty years is a long time.

Think about what you were doing 20 years ago. It seems like a lifetime ago. Twenty years ago, I was just graduating from undergraduate school. Now I have two children ages 13 and 9 and ten nieces and nephews that range in ages from 5-16.

With that thought in mind, I repeat: It took 20 years to get to the point in your home-loan term where the mortgage payment finally allocated more money towards paying down principal than to paying interest.

Before moving on, let's look at one more number.

$455,090.40

This number represents the future value of the loan for the lender or the <u>total amount</u> you will make in payments over the life of the loan.

$1,264.14 (monthly payment) x 360 (number of payments) = $455,090.40. This is the grand total of all of the payments over the 30-year period.

How much did the home owner in this example pay in <u>interest</u> over the life of the loan?

$455,090.40 - $200,000 = $255,090.40.

That's right—if this were your loan, you would have paid the bank more in interest than you paid for the home in the first place.

Keep these figures in mind as you read through the rest of this chapter and book.

MORTGAGE INTEREST AS A DAILY AMOUNT

So far, this chapter has covered the basics of mortgage math. Using some basic arithmetic, you can come up with a fairly reasonable estimate of the interest that would be charged annually and monthly on a mortgage.

Balance x Interest Rate = Annual Interest

Annual Interest / 12 = Monthly Interest

These calculations can now be taken one step further to calculate the amount of interest that is charged **each day** on a home loan.

Understanding this should make it easier to understand how the Home Equity Acceleration Plan (H.E.A.P.™) works to help you pay off your home loan years earlier.

Balance x Rate = Annual Interest

Annual Interest / 365 days a year = Daily Interest

For our example, it would look as follows:

$200,000 (balance) x .065 (rate) = $13,000 (annual interest)

$13,000 (annual interest) / 365 days = $35.62 **per day** in interest charges.

KEY POINT: INTEREST ACCRUES DAILY ON THE OUTSTANDING PRINCIPAL LOAN BALANCE.

Everything that you have read and learned so far indicates that, every time a mortgage payment is made, it first pays for the interest charges that have accrued **since the last payment.** After paying for those interest charges, any left-over amount is then applied towards the principal balance. If regularly scheduled payments are made, the lender receives the full potential value of the loan at the end of the term.

Now it's time to reveal a little more about the key point. Remember that monthly interest is calculated by the following equation:

Balance x Interest = Annual Interest

Annual Interest / 12 = Monthly Interest.

This is a good, simple way to figure out the average interest per month in our example loan. But what about February? February only has 28 days, so do you pay the same amount of interest in February as you do in March, which has 31 days?

The answer is no. Lenders take the interest calculation one step further and calculate the **daily interest**. To find the daily interest, the calculation would look like the following:

Balance x Interest = Annual Interest

Annual Interest / 365 = Daily Interest

Using the current example, the daily interest would be calculated as follows:

$200,000 (balance) x .065 (rate) = $13,000 (annual interest)

$13,000 (annual Interest) / 365 (days per year) = $35.62 (**daily interest**).

Having an understanding of daily interest is key to understanding how to efficiently accelerate paying off your mortgage.

MACRO INFORMATION ON MORTGAGES

When I first thought about putting this book together, I made a promise to myself to keep it under 150 pages. The concepts discussed, while very powerful, are not the most complicated and, therefore, I wanted to keep things short and simple.

I think I accomplished my goal of making the book simple and understandable. However, when I started to get the book ready for printing, I noticed that it turned out to be in excess of 150 pages.

In an effort to keep the promise I made to myself to keep the book under 150 pages, I have decided to put the 2nd half of this chapter online.

To download the remaining part of this chapter which will explain to you many useful items about mortgages (including the very powerful, misunderstood, and misused (and no longer available) 1% Cash Flow Arm (CFA) mortgage), please go to **www.HEAPlan.com**.

When you download the remaining part of this chapter, you can read about the following:

-Conventional Loans

-Amortization Schedules

-Types of Mortgages

    -Conventional and Governmental

    -FHA Loans

    -VA Loans

    -Conforming Loans

    -Jumbo Loans

    -B/C Loans

    -Fixed-Rate Mortgages

    -Balloon Loans

    -Adjustable Rate Mortgages (ARMs)

        -Margins

    -Negatively Amortizing Loans

-Mortgage Indexes

    -Constant Maturity Treasury (CMT) Indexes

    -12-Month Treasury Average (MTA)

    -London Inter Bank Offering Rates (LIBOR)

    -Prime Rate

-1% Cash Flow ARM Mortgage

-<u>Interest-only Loans</u>

If you have ever wondered if you have the "right" mortgage on your primary residence, you will want to read the 2nd part of this chapter which can be downloaded from the Internet. Because that information is not vital to understanding how H.E.A.P.™ works to pay down your mortgage years earlier, I've chosen to allow you to download it for FREE on the Internet instead of taking up space in this print version of the book.

SUMMARY ON MORTGAGES

While mortgages, in general, are not a difficult topic when dealing with Home Equity Management, you have to have a working knowledge of your mortgage options.

Knowledge is power; and even more importantly, by having a working knowledge of mortgages, you will not have to blindly take advice from advisors who may or may not have your best interest at heart.

With the basics covered, you are now ready to learn the various types of mortgage acceleration plans (including H.E.A.P.™)

Chapter 3
Traditional Mortgage Acceleration Plans

There are several programs out there to help people pay off their mortgage early. Let's take a closer look at the three most common programs and their effectiveness, their ease of use, and the ability to budget them into your current lifestyle.

After I tell you about the three programs, I'll introduce you to the most effective plan available, which goes by the name on the cover of this book—the Home Equity Acceleration Plan (H.E.A.P.™).

For all three plans, the following mortgage scenario will be used:

Original Loan Amount: $200,000
Loan Closing Date: December 31, 2010
First Payment Date: February 1, 2011
Interest Rate: 6.25%
Term: 30-Year Fixed
Payment: $1,231.43

---

1) ROUNDING UP

When you buy gasoline, do you try to squeeze the pump a few extra times in order to pay an even dollar amount?

For many, paying $39.68 doesn't affect them any more than paying $40.00 to fill up the automobile.

What about leaving a tip for your favorite server at a restaurant? If 15% of the bill comes out to $14.40, isn't it just easier to leave a $15.00 tip? Does leaving an extra 60-cent tip affect someone's daily life? Of course not.

This same mentality holds true for millions of people every month when they sit down to write the check for their mortgage payment.

Possibly the most common way people try to accelerate paying off their mortgage is by "Rounding Up" their payment to the nearest denomination of $10, $50, or $100.

Although this plan is both easy and affordable for most, it is the least structured of all the acceleration plans discussed in this book because the extra payment amount is not required. You just decide each month how much you want to round up the payment when you write out your check.

If you use direct withdrawals from your checking account to pay your mortgage, you may choose to add the extra amount when you set up the payment amount.

Most people who use this plan aren't really considering the exact effect it will have on their mortgage payoff date. It just seems like a good way to knock a few months off the term of the loan, and it isn't painful because of the low dollar amounts typically involved in Rounding Up.

When you consider using Rounding Up as a way to reduce the term of your mortgage, remember what you learned earlier about how interest is **charged in arrears and how payments are applied** when they are received by the bank.

Using our mortgage example, let's analyze the effect that "Rounding Up" the payments would have on the overall length of the term. First, let's take a look at the interest accrued in January 2011 and how much of the first payment would be applied towards the balance when **not** using Rounding Up:

Balance = $200,000

Daily interest = $34.25

Days in month = 31

Total Interest = $1,061.64

Payment = $1,231.43

Amount Applied to Principal = $169.79 ($1,231.43 – $1,061.64)

New Balance = $199,830.21 ($200,000 - $169.79)

Now remember that any **extra** payment amount will directly reduce the principal balance of the loan, which, in turn, reduces the amount of interest that will accrue and be charged each day of the next month.

This means that more and more of the payment will be applied toward the principal earlier in the loan term, and, as you will soon see, paying extra towards a mortgage early in the life of the loan significantly affects the total amount of interest paid over the life of the loan.

In the current example, a monthly payment of $1,231.43 on a $200,000 loan would pay off the loan as scheduled in 30 years. By simply rounding up the monthly payment to $1,240, $1,250 or $1,300, the borrower would be paying an additional amount of $8.57, $18.57, or $68.57 per month, respectively.

These amounts would be applied directly towards the principal loan balance, thereby reducing the interest charged in subsequent months and, ultimately, reducing the term of the loan.

The chart below shows how the additional payments would affect the term of the loan. Remember, this loan has its first payment due on February 1, 2011.

Monthly Payment	Additional Payment	Payoff Date	Total Interest Paid	Interest Saved
$1,231.43	$0.00	2/1/2041	$243,316	$0
$1,240.00	$8.57	7/1/2040	$237,514	**$5,802**
$1,250.00	$18.57	11/1/2039	$231,139	**$12,177**
$1,300.00	$68.57	2/1/2037	$204,368	**$38,948**

As you can see, simply rounding up the payment each month reduces the loan term and total interest charged. If you chose to round up to a $1,300 monthly payment, the <u>additional payments</u> would add up to approximately $822.84. However, this cost spread out over the period of a year is affordable and easy to budget.

While the additional amounts paid each month are not significant, you can see the power of paying just a few extra dollars each month and how it affects a long-term loan.

In the example, if you paid just $68.57 extra a month over the life of the loan, you would pay off the loan four years earlier and save nearly $40,000 in interest.

As you can see, Rounding Up is very affordable and simple. Paying an extra $8.57 or even $18.57 should not require any changes to most peoples' monthly budgets. Even an additional $68.57 is affordable for most. Think about it. You can't even go to dinner today at a nice restaurant with your spouse and one or two children and drop less than $60.00.

As I mentioned in the beginning of this chapter, the goal is to show you the "real" math so that you can make decisions about which concepts in this book are best for your situation. To do that, let's take a closer look at the actual dollars spent and the dollars saved for each of these rounded-up payment options.

Monthly Payment Amount	$1,231.43	$1,240	$1,250	$1,300
Number of Payments	360	353	344	312
Total of ALL Payments	$443,316.38	$437,770	$431,250	$405,600
Actual Savings	**$0.00**	**$5,802.40**	**$12,177.68**	**$38,948.01**

Rounding Up is an easy, inexpensive way to reduce the total term and the total payments of your mortgage. Millions of people do it every month without even knowing the exact effect it will have on their loan.

Should you be using Rounding Up to reduce the term of your mortgage? It depends. The other strategies you will read about in this chapter are better than Rounding Up for accelerating your mortgage, and Equity Harvesting (which you can read about in Chapter 6) is a much better way to build wealth than paying down your mortgage; but if the choice is between doing nothing and Rounding Up, you should use Rounding Up.

2) APPLYING THE BONUS

Annually, millions of people receive some type of cash bonus. This could be from an employer, from a rich uncle, a parent who has passed away, or even from the Federal Government in the form of an income tax refund. Although a tax refund isn't truly a bonus, to many people, it feels like one.

For this section of the chapter, let's assume you will **receive an annual income tax refund**. No bonus is guaranteed from an employer, the IRS, or other sources; but in order to have an example that makes sense, I'll assume a systematic tax refund.

To compare this method to the other common "pay off your mortgage early" methods, we'll use the same terms: a $200,000 mortgage at a rate of 6.25%, a 30-year term, and a payment of $1,231.43, with the first one being due February 1, 2011.

Let's also assume you earn $60,000 a year, and, as a savings plan, you have the maximum income tax withheld from your paycheck, knowing that there will be a sizable income tax refund the following year. Let's assume that the refund in this example is **$1,000** a year and will continue to be a similar amount for the life of the 30-year home loan.

Although you would love to spend the entire tax refund amount on new electronic equipment or a vacation, you are dedicated to using the refund each year to reduce the term of your home mortgage. Therefore, you will apply the $1,000 refund towards the mortgage, as an extra payment that will be paid to the lender on May 1 of every year during the term of the loan.

Look what happens to your mortgage when you apply the extra $1,000 payment each year.

Payment	Additional Pmt	Payoff Date	Total Interest Paid	Interest Saved
$1,231.43	$0.00	2/1/2041	$243,316.00	$0.00
$1,231.43	$1,000.00	5/1/2033	$196,968.00	**$46,348.00**

Uncle Sam, through tax refund checks, has helped you reduce the term of the loan by almost five years, which saved you over $46,000 in interest charges over the life of the loan.

That's pretty much it with Applying the Bonus. It's simple and easy, although it's not going to help you pay off your mortgage 10-15+ years early.

Now consider this though: What if you "Round Up" **and** apply the bonus? For this scenario, let's assume the same $1,000 annual refund and a monthly payment of $1,250, which is an additional $18.57 each month.

Monthly Payment	Additional Monthly Payment	Additional Annual Payment	Payoff Date	Total Interest Paid	Interest Saved
$1,231.43	$0.00	0	2/1/2041	$243,316.00	$0.00
$1,250.00	$18.57	$1,000	5/01/2035	$189,355.00	**$53,961.00**

By combining these two simple methods of term reduction and keeping it affordable for you, the term would be reduced to 24 years and 4 months; and your total interest savings would be $53,961.

While the Bonus Plan seems simple and certainly can work, what would be better advice for you?

Assuming you have the discipline to do so, it would be better for you to take home as much money as possible from your salary/paycheck from work and pay down more of the mortgage with that extra money each month (even if this causes you to owe money to the IRS when you file your tax return).

Why would anyone want to use an IRS tax refund as a savings plan? (Hundreds of thousands of Americans do this knowingly or unknowingly each year). The IRS does not pay interest on the refund and letting the IRS keep your money throughout the year is not a good financial decision.

Let's see how it would affect your loan to apply your extra take-home income to your loan each month instead of giving it to the IRS.

Assume that instead of missing out on an additional income of $83.33 a month ($83.33 x 12 = $1,000) that is being withheld from your paycheck, you instead receive that money each month to do with as you see fit.

Then let's assume that you go even further and change the amount withheld from your paycheck so that you will actually owe $1,000 when filing your tax return next year. That gives you another $83.33 per month in your paycheck (or an additional $1,000 a year).

The end result is that, instead of having $83.33 removed from your check every month, you would have an additional $166.66 in your paycheck ($2,000 a year).

Now let's assume that you add the extra $166.66 to your mortgage payment each month. By restructuring the withholding amount and applying that amount directly to the mortgage monthly payment, you would save **$75,483** over the life of the loan in interest charges.

The following chart summarizes the savings. The figures in Row 2 illustrate how much interest is saved using Rounding Up and applying the $1,000 tax refund bonus each year towards the mortgage. Row 3 shows the effect of having $166.66 less withheld from your paycheck without the use of Rounding Up.

Monthly Payment	Additional Monthly Payment	Additional Annual Payment	Payoff Date	Total Interest Paid	Interest Saved
$1,231.43	$0.00	0.00	2/1/2041	$243,316.00	$0.00
$1,250.00	$18.57	1,000	5/1/2035	$189,355.00	$53,961.00
$1,398.09	$166.66	0.00	2/1/2033	$167,832.93	$75,483.45

You may be saying to yourself that you now have to find additional income to pay the income tax bill each April. That's right, and the following material will show you how to find that money using the Home Equity Acceleration Plan.

3) BI-WEEKLY PLANS

Most mortgage payments are due on the first day of every month. When this payment is made, the previous month's interest that has accrued is paid. Therefore, if the previous month had 30 days, interest on the loan would have been accruing for 30 days.

Since there are twelve months in a year, there are twelve mortgage payments due every year. Going back to our example of a $200,000 mortgage amortized at a 6.25% interest rate, twelve monthly payments of $1,231.43 would add up to an annual payment total of $14,777.16.

Today, many homeowners are utilizing a program that is offered through many loan servicers (and also through many private companies). This program is most commonly known as the Bi-Weekly payment program. This program allows borrowers to make one half of their required monthly payment every two weeks. So on February 1, instead of paying the typical monthly payment of **$1,231.43**, a payment of **$615.72** is made. Then, two weeks later, another payment of **$615.72** is made.

Let's use our basic math skills to help us determine how and why this program works to reduce the term of a mortgage.

How many weeks are there in a year? 52.

If a payment is made every two weeks, how many half payments are made per year? 26.

Since the payment amount is half of the full amount, how many full payments are made per year? 13.

This is one more payment per year than a borrower would normally pay by making monthly payments.

So the main reason the term of the mortgage is reduced is because an extra mortgage payment is made every year. As with Rounding Up or the Bonus Plan, anytime you pay more than is required on your mortgage, it lowers the principal balance and the interest due (which will cut months or years off the term of the loan).

Most of the Bi-Weekly payment programs require direct withdrawal from a bank account to make it easier on the customer and to make sure that payments are received by the day they are to be posted.

Let's see what the actual numbers look like on our $200,000 mortgage example.

Year	Bi-Weekly Payment $615.72 Year End Balance	Payment for 30-year Amortization $1,231.43 Year End Balance
1	$196,629.76	$197,656.46
2	$193,060.32	$195,162.18
3	$189,279.91	$192,507.46
4	$185,276.03	$189,681.97
5	$181,035.53	$186,674.75
6	$176,544.36	$183,474.10
7	$171,787.75	$180,067.58
8	$166,749.98	$176,441.96
9	$163,726.63	$172,583.14
10	$161,414.43	$168,476.10
11	$155,763.54	$164,104.89
12	$149,778.63	$159,452.52
13	$143,439.97	$154,500.87
14	$129,616.49	$149,230.75
15	$122,086.10	$143,621.63
16	$114,110.61	$137,651.74
17	$105,663.71	$131,297.85
18	$96,717.57	$124,565.25
19	$83,546.92	$117,337.69
20	$77,207.69	$109,667.16
21	$66,579.57	$101,523.90
22	$55,323.26	$92,846.19
23	$43,401.65	$83,610.32
24	$30,775.34	$73,780.38
25	$17,402.74	$63,318.16
26	$ 3,239.73	$52,183.02
27		$40,331.61
28		$27,717.91
29		$14,292.88
30		$0

Let's compare the numbers.

Payment Program	Monthly Payment	Loan Balance at 5 Years	Total Interest Paid over 30 Years	Interest Saved
Standard Monthly	$1,231.43	$186,674.75	$243,319.13	$0.00
Bi-weekly	$615.72	$181,035.53	$187,473.64	$55,845.49

The chart above shows that the Bi-Weekly payment program saved $55,845.49 in interest charges over the entire term of the loan. This interest savings would reduce the length of the term to just over 26 years; that's almost a 5-year reduction.

The chart also details the balance <u>after Year 5</u>. The reason this number was included is that, although most people want to aggressively pay off their mortgage, they will, in all likelihood, sell their home or refinance the mortgage within five years. If you didn't know, in the U.S., mortgages are kept for an average of 3-5 years. With this in mind, it is just as important to identify the 5-year savings as it is to identify the savings over the entire term.

The chart shows that, if you use the Bi-Weekly payment program, you owe $181,035.53 at the end of the 5th year, whereas if you use the standard monthly payment program, you would owe $186,674.75. This means that you would have about $5,640 (not including appreciation) of additional equity.

If you get a calculator out, you will see that 26 payments of $615.72 total annual payments of $16,008.72 or an additional $1,231.56.

This equates to approximately one additional payment per year. However, the Bi-Weekly program **works better because you would be applying principal twice a month**, which reduces the **daily interest** paid every time a payment is posted.

Using the same example, the interest on the original $200,000 mortgage would be accruing at approximately $34.25 ($200,000 x .0625 (rate) / 365 days/year = $34.25) per day during the first month. By paying $615.72 (half of the normal monthly payment) on the 15th of the first month, the accrued interest of

$513.75 ($34.25 x 15) would be paid, and $101.97 ($615.72 – $513.75) would be applied to the principal.

This means that, for the remaining days of the month, interest would only be charged on $199,898.03, rather than the full $200,000, <u>reducing the daily interest charged</u>.

In other words, instead of the interest accruing for 30 days on $200,000, it would only accrue for two weeks on $200,000; then, when the $615.72 payment is made, the interest would begin to accrue on the smaller principal balance of $199,898.03 for the next two weeks.

When the next payment is made, that payment would slightly reduce the principal balance again. As you continue to do this every two weeks, it would slowly reduce the overall debt, which, in turn, would reduce the daily interest charged that over time increases the speed at which the loan is paid in full. Although the reduction of the principal balance is minimal, the compounding effect over time is significant and makes the plan beneficial to borrowers who use the program.

Applying the funds

Earlier, I mentioned that there are many private companies who offer this service (most at a minimal charge). These companies handle the setup and the general accounting for customers who want to take advantage of it.

<u>**Some**</u> of these companies **will not** apply the funds immediately to the mortgage account and will instead wait **until the end of the year** and then apply the extra payment. This will shorten the term of the loan as well (simply because you are making an extra payment each year), however, not by as much as if the payments were applied immediately.

If the extra payments aren't applied immediately, the interest will continue to accrue on higher principal balances throughout the year. These higher principal balances will persist until the extra payment (and the resultant principal reduction) is made.

What I'm saying here is that, if you opt for a program like this, you should know when the company applies the payments and should even go as far as to ask for the amortization schedule and the annual accounting statement from the company. This annual accounting statement should show their account activity for the most recent periods. This information will tell you whether the payments are being applied immediately.

It is good to know that there are several variations of this program; some have even set the program to run **weekly**.

What you'll find interesting is that there is virtually no difference between making Weekly and Bi-Weekly payments. If you make weekly payments, you would make 52 payments annually of $307.86, which adds up to $16,008.72. Since the payment is ¼ of the monthly payment, the borrower is still only making the equivalent of 13 full monthly payments (52 / 4). The annual payment amount is only a few cents more than the bi-weekly annual payment of $16,008.59. Therefore, the term is virtually identical when comparing the weekly payment to bi-weekly plan would.

As I mentioned earlier, most of these plans require a system of direct withdrawals from a checking or savings account. Should there ever be a significant change in your income, you would have to notify the company handling the transactions and have the payments stopped. However, you would still need to continue making at least the monthly payments that are due.

SUMMARY ON THE "COMMON" MORTGAGE ACCELERATION PLANS

So far, we have covered the three common mortgage acceleration plans. We have covered the **Rounding Up** method in which the customer adds a few extra dollars each month to their mortgage payment, which can reduce the mortgage term by a few years (which is better than doing nothing).

We have also covered how applying a one-time payment per year (**Applying the Bonus**) utilizes a lump-sum approach which can reduce the term once again by a few years (again better than doing nothing and can be used in combination with the Rounding Up method).

45

The **Bi-Weekly** payment method also reduces the term by essentially making an extra payment throughout the course of the year by paying every two weeks and by reducing the principal balance more frequently.

All of these plans, although easy to budget, will only reduce the term of the mortgage by 2 – 7 years. While paying off a home loan in 23-28 years is better than paying it off in 30 years, what if there was another plan that allowed a borrower to cut the term in half (or more) without altering their spending habits?

Chapter 4
The Home Equity Acceleration Plan
(H.E.A.P.™)

Is it a fair statement to say that there are two types of people in this world?

There are those who want to use the equity in their homes to build a tax-favorable retirement nest egg, and there are those who want to pay off the debt on their home as soon as possible.

What you will learn in this chapter is a unique program that will show you how to accomplish the life-long dream of becoming mortgage debt free and even totally debt free.

WHAT IS H.E.A.P.™?

-H.E.A.P.™ is a dynamic new financial plan that enables you to pay off your home mortgage several years early **without** changing your normal spending habits.

-It is **NOT** a Bi-Weekly payment plan or some other extra payment plan or scheme.

-YOU are **completely in control** of the whole plan at all times.

-Once properly budgeted, H.E.A.P.™ is a **simple plan** that can be set up in, literally, a matter of days.

-H.E.A.P.™ is also a plan that has **NO downside and NO risk**.

-H.E.A.P.™ is a plan where many homeowners will **pay off their mortgage 10+ years early** and save, on average, over $100,000 in mortgage interest.

After the above statements, I imagine you are as ready and excited to read the following chapter as any chapter of any book you've ever read. While H.E.A.P.™ will not bring us world peace, it is a unique program that I think you'll really enjoy reading about and potentially implement for yourself.

WHO DOES H.E.A.P.™ WORK FOR?

There are two prerequisites you must have in order to use H.E.A.P.™ to pay down your mortgage in the most expedient manner possible.

1) **You must have equity in your home** (you'll understand why in the upcoming pages).

2) **You need to make more money than you spend**. I'm sorry, but I've not yet run across a mortgage or debt acceleration plan to help you pay down debt sooner if you don't earn more than you spend.

I will also show you later in this chapter how you can use H.E.A.P.™ to your advantage even if you happen to spend "exactly" what you earn every month.

Why have you never heard of H.E.A.P.™?

H.E.A.P.™ is not a new concept, but it is relatively unknown. Why it is unknown is a bit of a long story; but, generally speaking, mortgage professionals are not taught this program in the educational programs available in the U.S. marketplace and banks don't know anything about it.

Traditionally speaking, mortgage professionals sell mortgages; they do not craft plans or help clients figure out ways to reduce the term of their mortgage. The same goes for banks. Since the vast majority of financial planners, insurance agents, CPAs/EAs/accountants, and attorneys know very little about mortgages in general (let alone mortgage acceleration plans), homeowners are not receiving information on this very unique and simple mortgage-reduction plan.

Ask yourself the following question:

If you could pay off your mortgage substantially sooner than 30 years (assuming you have a 30-year mortgage) and you wouldn't have to alter your spending habits – would you?

The question is more of a rhetorical question as the obvious answer is "Yes." If one of your advisors asked you this question, I'm sure you would follow up the question with, "Can you show me how to do that?"

How in the world can a homeowner pay off their mortgage "substantially sooner" and not change their spending habits?

It can be done through the creative use of a **Home Equity Line Of Credit (HELOC)**.

FUNDAMENTALS THAT YOU NEED TO LEARN IN ORDER TO UNDERSTAND HOW AND WHY H.E.A.P.™ WORKS

1) You **earn zero** on your average checking account balances;

2) Interest is **charged daily** on your loans; and

3) Home mortgage interest is **paid in arrears** (both 2) and 3) were discussed in Chapter 2).

Is it fair to say that most Americans keep a balance in their personal checking accounts?

Absolutely.

Those who don't are not in a positive cash-flow situation and should worry about simply making their monthly mortgage payment rather than trying to find creative ways to pay it off early.

Depending on the person, the average monthly checking account balance is anywhere from $500 to as much as $5,000+. People use this money to pay their monthly bills (gas, food, utilities, clothes, travel, entertainment, and, yes, the mortgage expense).

What's the problem with a checking account?

Most people **earn NO interest** on money in a personal checking account. If you do earn interest on such accounts, it is very low; and it is taxable every year.

Therefore, if you are lucky enough to earn 1-2% annually on your checking account balance, in the 30% income tax bracket (state and federal), you would net .7%-1.4% annually after taxes.

This number is close enough to zero that, for purposes of this book, I will assume that all readers earn zero on the balances they carry in their checking accounts.

<u>What does that mean, and who cares?</u>

Everyone should care; and the analogy to illustrate why comes from the previous material on mortgage debt. Most readers do not like the notion that banks earn money daily as they charge borrowers interest on their mortgages.

If that's true, then why don't we get upset that banks are not crediting us daily interest (in a positive manner) on money in our checking accounts (even if it is taxable)?

We should; and, in the upcoming material, you will see first-hand how H.E.A.P.™ will help you use "**every available dollar every day**" to pay down mortgage debt (which is the best use of money in a checking account).

HOME EQUITY LINE OF CREDIT

Most people know what a **Home Equity Line of Credit** (HELOC) is, and many have had one at one point in their lives. A HELOC is similar to a revolving line of credit—you can go to a lender and use the equity in your home to receive a "line of credit."

Aside from a small annual fee in some cases, if you are not accessing the line of credit, the beginning balance on the HELOC is **$0**.

Since the monthly payment due on a HELOC is based on the outstanding loan balance, if the HELOC has a balance of $0, there will be no monthly payment due.

After the HELOC is set up, you are literally given checks that can be used to access the equity line of the loan. In the traditional use of a HELOC, a borrower who is fixing up his/her house and doesn't have the cash to do so might go down to the local hardware store to buy building supplies and would use a check from the HELOC to pay for them.

When checks are used, interest starts on the HELOC and a monthly second mortgage payment is then due based on the amount of money borrowed.

If the HELOC balance is $10,000, the monthly payment is calculated by using the current interest rate and the number of days in the period.

If the interest rate is 8.25%, the payment for a 30-day month would be calculated as $10,000 x .0825 = 825 / 365 x 30 (days in current month) = $67.81.

This would be the interest due for the month. Some accounts have a 1% minimum, which would require a payment of $100.00 ($10,000 x .01). In this case, if $100.00 were paid, $32.19 would be applied to principal leaving a remaining balance of $9,967.81.

The "available credit" offered by a lender through a HELOC may be drawn when needed. Like a traditional home loan, the borrower must pay monthly payments and is required to pay off the balance over a specified period of time. And, like a mortgage, the **interest accrues daily** on the balance owed. When a payment is made, it is applied first to the interest due; and then any amount in excess of the interest is applied directly to the principal balance.

Many of these accounts are set up with "**interest only**" payment requirements with a limited "draw period" followed by a repayment period. Typical HELOCs have a ten-year draw period, after which normal payments are calculated to pay off the balance over the remainder of the term, which can be up to 30 years.

The interest rate for a HELOC is usually a variable (adjustable) rate. The measuring index or variable portion of the loan will often be the current prime interest rate. The "margin," or the fixed portion, will be an amount that the lender adds to the rate in accordance with the risk factors associated with the loan.

For example: A Line of Credit that leaves the borrower with little or no equity will have a higher "margin" than a line that leaves a large equity position. Generally speaking, a borrower with bad credit will have a higher "margin" charged to the loan; and someone with good credit can sometimes find a HELOC at the prime rate with no "margin" (and sometimes even less than the prime rate).

If the prime rate is 8.25% and the margin is zero, the rate on a HELOC at prime + 0 would be 8.25%. The rate on a HELOC is usually higher than that of a conventional fixed-rate mortgage (which does not use prime as a basis for the lending rate).

The following chart represents the historical data of the prime rate since the year 2001. As you can see, the rate has been as high as 8.5% and as low as 3.5% (which it is at the time of publication in 2011). There is no limit as to how long the rate can stay at one point or how often it can change. The prime rate is defined by the Wall Street Journal (WSJ) as *"The base rate on corporate loans posted by at least 75% of the nation's 30 largest banks."* It is not the "best" rate offered by banks.

Date of Change	Prime Rate	Date of Change	Prime Rate
1-Feb-01	8.50%	30-Jun-05	6.25%
21-Mar-01	8.00%	9-Aug-05	6.50%
19-Apr-01	7.50%	20-Sep-05	6.75%
16-May-01	7.00%	1-Nov-05	7.00%
28-Jun-01	6.75%	13-Dec-05	7.25%
22-Aug-01	6.50%	31-Jan-06	7.50%
18-Sep-01	6.00%	28-Mar-06	7.75%
3-Oct-01	5.50%	10-May-06	8.00%
7-Nov-01	5.00%	29-Jun-06	8.25%
12-Dec-01	4.75%	31-Oct-07	7.50%
7-Nov-02	4.25%	31-Oct-07	7.50%
27-Jun-03	4.00%	11-Dec-07	7.25%
11-Aug-04	4.50%	22-Jan-08	6.50%
22-Sep-04	4.75%	30-Jan-08	6.00%
10-Nov-04	5.00%	18-Mar-08	5.25%
14-Dec-04	5.25%	30-Apr-08	5.00%
2-Feb-05	5.50%	8-Oct-08	4.50%
22-Mar-05	5.75%	30-Oct-08	4.00%
3-May-05	6.00%	16-Dec-08	3.25%

When you learn how H.E.A.P.™ works, you need to keep in mind that the amount of debt carried in a HELOC is minor; and the interest rate on the HELOC will not have a huge affect on the overall time it takes to pay down your total mortgage or other debt.

When a HELOC is mentioned to most borrowers, they will usually think of it as a second mortgage. In fact, that is the way most of them are set up; however, some lenders now do offer first lien lines of credit.

Generally speaking, so long as the HELOC loan balance does not exceed $100,000 and the borrower has no other home equity debt on the property, the interest on the loan is tax deductible (except as limited by Section 264(a) of the IRC).

Before securing a "typical" HELOC, you need to know something very important. By securing a HELOC, you are using available equity of the house. When you draw funds from the HELOC, you reduce the equity in your home; it can even be reduced to $0.00 if you access all of the equity.

For example: If the first mortgage on your home is $80,000 and the HELOC balance is $20,000, there would be a $100,000 lien against your home. If the home is valued at $105,000, you would only have $5,000 in available equity. This is not necessarily a negative thing; however, if your goal is to list and sell the house within a year, it could potentially cost you money to sell the house (because the house would be sold in a negative equity situation when you take into account realtor fees and other closing costs).

In general, a HELOC is a type of mortgage that gives you the flexibility to use available equity when you need it and only pay for what you are using. With a better understanding of how a HELOC works, it will now be easier to understand the concept of H.E.A.P.™.

H.E.A.P.™ HAS TWO PARTS THAT HELP YOU PAY DOWN MORTGAGE DEBT.

1) H.E.A.P.™ WORKS <u>IN CONJUNCTION</u> WITH A HELOC.

As stated earlier, H.E.A.P.™ will show you how to use "**every available dollar every day**" to pay down mortgage debt.

How?

Through the use of a HELOC that you will ultimately **use as your checking account**.

First, you set up a HELOC utilizing the equity in your home. The HELOC is usually a second lien on your personal residence. For the first example, I will assume that the line of credit you can access is **$25,000**.

The repayment terms are interest only, and the rate is variable tied to prime. Although it is not a realistic assumption, we will assume that prime remains at 8.25% for the term (prime will go up or down over time). I only assume this to make the concept easier to understand.

As noted in the previous chart, the prime rate can fluctuate several times per year. In the past several years, it has been as low as 3.5% and as high as 8.5%.

Now I am going to pretend the example homeowner is in several different situations so you can see first-hand how H.E.A.P.™ can work to save you tens of thousands to more than $100,000 in mortgage interest over the life of a loan.

<u>EXAMPLE 1:</u>

In this example, I'm going to assume that you have a "middle-class" income. You are very serious about paying down your mortgage and you are being "frugal" to pay it down as quickly as possible.

I'm going to assume that you just bought a **new home** and, therefore, you are implementing H.E.A.P.™ with a new 30-year mortgage.

You have the following income and expenses:

-Monthly income (**after taxes**) = $5,000

-First mortgage balance = $200,000 (30-year mortgage)

-First payment due date = Feb. 1, 2008

-Monthly mortgage payment at 6.25% = $1,231.43

-HELOC interest rate = 8.25%

-All other monthly payments (bills, credit cards, utilities, etc.) = $1,650.00

-Miscellaneous monthly expenditures (dinners, movies, fuel, etc.) = $800

-Total monthly outlay = **$3,681.43**

For this example, I'm going to assume you will **NOT** consolidate any other bills into the HELOC (like credit card debt, etc.).

Once you are fully educated on this plan, you will most likely want to consolidate other debt using the HELOC.

Why?

Because interest payments on credit card charges are NOT deductible whereas, when set up correctly, interest payments on a HELOC are.

Once the HELOC is opened, a comfortable amount of emergency cash is determined. This is the amount of money that you should have available at all times in the line of credit. This amount will then be available to you in case of an emergency.

Therefore, with this example, I'll assume you should have $15,000 available at all times in the HELOC in case of an emergency. This amount was determined by taking three months of your salary. There is no standard amount that is required as a reserve. You will need to determine for yourself what an acceptable reserve amount is considering your own situation. The reserve is really there to pay your bills should you become disabled, lose your job, or have an unexpected expense (like a major health expense) for a short period of time.

Having said that, it is usually recommended that you reserve three times your after-tax income (in this example, that is $15,000).

If I assume that you are designating $15,000 of the $25,000 HELOC as a cushion available for emergencies, this will leave you with $10,000 at your disposal from the HELOC to be used to pay down mortgage debt with H.E.A.P.™.

USING A HELOC TO PAY DOWN THE PIMARY MORTGAGE DEBT

When you access the HELOC, instead of spending borrowed funds to fix up the house, take a vacation, or otherwise use the money for miscellaneous expenses, you will use the HELOC money to pay **down the debt on the primary mortgage**.

In this example, you will draw **$10,000** from the HELOC and **pay it directly towards the first mortgage**.

Remember, H.E.A.P.™ is designed to help you pay off your primary mortgage several years early; and the money from the HELOC will be used to accomplish that goal.

By paying $10,000 down on the first mortgage, you will obviously reduce the principal of the first mortgage (and the interest that would have been paid on the loan over the long term) and shorten the length of your primary mortgage.

Having made this payment on your first mortgage, you now will have to pay at least the minimum payment on the new $10,000 HELOC. **The key, as you will see with H.E.A.P.™, is how quickly a client can pay down the $10,000 HELOC**.

Remember, once H.E.A.P.™ is budgeted correctly, you will NOT have to change your spending habits, which is why this is such a useful program.

The "**total**" **debt** on the home is **still the same** as the day the HELOC is accessed ($190,000 left on the primary mortgage and $10,000 from the HELOC that was applied to pay down the first mortgage).

HOW H.E.A.P.™ WORKS TO USE "<u>EVERY AVAILABLE DOLLAR EVERY DAY</u>" TO PAY DOWN MORTGAGE DEBT

After you obtain and access your HELOC, **you will have your paychecks (and any other "income")** <u>deposited directly</u> **into the line of credit account (NOT your normal checking account)**.

You might want to think about that for just a minute since it's vital to understanding the mechanics of H.E.A.P.™.

Normally, you deposit earned and unearned income and other deposits into your personal checking accounts. What does that earn you annually as an investment rate of return? **<u>ZERO</u>**.

Ask yourself the following question:

When you deposit your paycheck and other deposits in the **<u>HELOC</u>**, what rate of return are you earning on that money?

Zero, like money in your checking account?

<u>NO!</u>

You are effectively earning the rate of return of the HELOC which in our example is 8.25%.

When you deposit your paycheck and other deposits into the HELOC, what in essence are you doing?

You are using "**<u>every available dollar every day</u>**" to pay down mortgage debt.

If the HELOC interest rate is higher than the primary mortgage rate, most borrowers will mentally equate the pre-tax investment rate of return on money deposited in the HELOC as the same as the primary mortgage (6.25% in our example).

Which brings up the question: Now that you have deposited all of your income into a HELOC, **how will you pay your bills**?

The answer is amazingly simple, and you've probably figured it out—**<u>you will pay your bills by writing checks out of your HELOC account</u>**.

Most people are not aware that there are HELOC accounts that can literally function as a checking account. After you set up the account, you are given checks to use so you can access the line of credit to pay bills.

In this example, you would pay the **$3,681.43** in total monthly bills by writing checks from your HELOC just as you would from a normal checking account. You can choose to write one **$3,681.43** check to your primary checking account (and then pay your bills from there) or simply use HELOC checks to pay each bill.

RUNNING THE NUMBERS

Let's look at the running balance for the first few months of the line of credit where you deposit your paycheck into the HELOC account. This should really crystallize for you how the H.E.A.P.™ process works from a logistical manner.

Assume that you get paid on the 15th and the 30th of each month. Remember, with this example, you started out by accessing the HELOC in the amount of $10,000, which you used to pay down the mortgage balance on your first home loan. This started the HELOC with a "balance owed" of $10,000 and available funds of $15,000 in the line of credit.

Remember, our goal is to keep a minimum of $15,000 available at all times in the HELOC for emergency funds. Also, remember that you are earning income above what you spend on normal household bills (which creates a positive average balance in a normal checking account that earns virtually no interest each year).

Date	Activity	Amount	Balance	Avail Credit
2/1/2011	1st Mtg Reduction	($10,000)	$10,000	$15,000
2/15/2011	Payroll Deposit	$2,500	$7,562.50	$17,438
2/28/2011	Payroll Deposit	$2,500	$5,109.77	$19,890
3/1/2011	Bills	($3,681.43)	$8,791.20	$16,209
3/15/2011	Payroll Deposit	$2,500	$6,346.14	$18,654
3/30/2011	Payroll Deposit	$2,500	$3,885.80	$21,114
4/1/2011	Bills	($3,681.43)	$7,567.23	$17,433
4/15/2011	Payroll Deposit	$2,500	$5,114.53	$19,885
4/30/2011	Payroll Deposit	$2,500	$2,646.49	$22,354
5/1/2011	Bills	($3,681.43)	$6,327.92	$18,672
5/15/2011	Payroll Deposit	$2,500	$3,867.47	$21,133
5/30/2011	Payroll Deposit	$2,500	$1,391.65	$23,608
6/1/2011	Bills	($3,681.43)	$5,073.08	$19,927
6/15/2011	Payroll Deposit	$2,500	$2,604.78	$22,395
6/30/2011	Payroll Deposit	$2,500	$121.06	$24,879
7/1/2011	Bills	($3,681.43)	$3,802.49	$21,198
7/15/2011	Payroll Deposit	$2,500	$1,326.26	$23,674
7/30/2011	Payroll Deposit	$2,500	**HELCO PAYOFF**	Access another $10k

In five months, without changing any spending habits, you just paid off the $10,000 balance on your HELOC.

Besides smiling due to the fact that the HELOC has been paid off, what do you do next to continue using H.E.A.P.™?

You guessed it—you will write another HELOC check for $10,000 to pay down your first mortgage again. Then you will continue with life as usual, except that your paycheck will continue to be deposited in the HELOC.

THE NUMBERS

Understand that the exact numbers are not that important due to the fact that everyone's situation will be different. It's the concept that either does or does not work.

This concept will work for people who <u>have the discipline</u> to use it and who carry some kind of balance monthly in their checking accounts.

Sure, those who use H.E.A.P.™ are going to have unexpected expenses or expected expenses that will change the numbers in any given period of time.

The key is that you are always using your money in its **best use**—and having money sitting in a checking account earning little to no interest (which is taxable each year) is **NOT** in your best interest.

Back to the example

In order to make the program a success, it is extremely important that you anticipate the "other" expenses that you have incurred in the past and budget those into your H.E.A.P.™ calculations.

In this example, you will be able to pay down the $10,000 HELOC approximately 2.4 times a year. You will do this automatically without thinking or extra work by using the HELOC as a checking account.

You simply live your life, and H.E.A.P.™ allows you to use "**every available dollar every day**" to pay down mortgage debt.

Additionally, at the end of each month, H.E.A.P.™ automatically applied the "**surplus**" to pay down HELOC debt.

The "**surplus**" is defined as what you normally would have had left in a traditional checking account at the end of the month. As you will probably agree, most of the American public figures out a way to spend most of, if not all, of the "**surplus**" that is left in a checking account at the end of the month (usually on miscellaneous items that are NOT needed).

After **PROPER** budgeting, in this example you paid down the HELOC 2.4 times a year WITHOUT changing your spending habits so long as you choose to have the discipline to stay with the plan.

If you are telling yourself that you will have other expenses that will not allow such a high "**surplus**" to be created at the end of the month, that may be true; but again, that gets back to proper budgeting when setting up H.E.A.P.™.

With **YOUR** particular plan, you are in charge of the budgeting; and when you sit down with your H.E.A.P.™ advisor, the numbers will be as "real world" as you make them.

You know what they say: "Garbage in, garbage out." So make sure you are conservative with your budgeting to get a real-world proposal from your H.E.A.P.™ advisor.

How much total interest was saved in Example 1 as budgeted using H.E.A.P.™?

Months Paid	Months Saved	Years Paid	Years Saved	Interest Paid	Interest Saved
103	**257**	**8.6**	**21.4**	**$58,064**	**$185,254**

Summary: This example client paid off ALL mortgage debt in 8.6 years vs. 30 years and saved **$185,254** in mortgage interest in the process.

Not bad, if I do say so myself. This is the power of H.E.A.P.™ and the reason many people will gravitate to it for help in ridding themselves of mortgage debt.

Are you a H.E.A.P.™ expert yet?

Probably not, but you should be starting to get the hang of how the plan works. If you are like most readers, you are also quite intrigued, and are wondering how much money the plan can save you over the life of your mortgage.

Let's go back and make sure you understand the calculations used in the table illustrating the $10,000 HELOC pay down.

The HELOC balance started at $10,000 (and that borrowed money was used to pay down the primary mortgage from $200,000 to $190,000).

Then you put in a paycheck of $2,500 on the 15th and again on the 30th of the month. Mentally you would think that the HELOC balance before expenses that are paid on the 1st of the following month would be $5,000 even. It's not, because there is "daily interest" due on the balance of the debt in the HELOC.

Therefore, in this example, the HELOC balance at the end of one month is $5,109.77, not $5,000, even though you might think it should be.

As the months go by, the HELOC amount will go down and up as checks are deposited and money is withdrawn to pay bills.

When the balance in the HELOC reaches a point at which the next paycheck or deposit will bring the HELOC amount to zero or less, it is then time to re-access the HELOC for X amount of dollars so the HELOC balance increases again to the starting point of $10,000 in our example.

The following is a chart you would receive from a H.E.A.P.™ advisor as part of your custom three-page report. The report would have all of the specific numbers from the chart including how long it would take to pay off your mortgage using H.E.A.P.™ and how much mortgage interest you would save over the life of the plan (like the 8.6 years and $185,254 respectively in Example 1).

The large black bars represent how long it takes to pay off a 30-year mortgage. The white bars represent how long it takes to pay off the mortgage with H.E.A.P.™. The small black bars in the front left part of the chart represent the $10,000 HELOC.

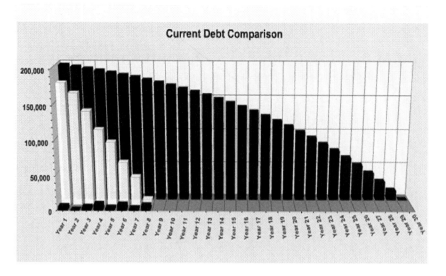

CRITICS AND/OR SKEPTICS OF H.E.A.P.™?

The biggest critics and skeptics of the program will key in on one fact—that the average American who uses the program will not be depositing ANY money into a savings or brokerage account to build a "retirement nest egg."

In other words, if the client uses H.E.A.P.™, he/she will not have any other money left over to fund traditional retirement vehicles such as 401(k) plans or IRAs or an after-tax brokerage account.

Such criticism is misplaced.

Remember, the goal in using H.E.A.P.™ is to pay off the home mortgage as quickly as possible; and, in the example, "you" did it in just under nine years. You saved **$185,254** in interest over the life of the plan.

IF you want to also have an additional savings or retirement plan at or outside of work, then **that amount needs to be budgeted into your monthly expenses** when starting H.E.A.P.™. (This would reduce the amount that could be allocated to pay down the HELOC and, in turn, total mortgage debt).

You need to keep in mind that the goal of people who use H.E.A.P.™ is to pay off their home mortgage as soon as possible.

People who want to build the largest possible pre- and post-tax retirement nest egg are NOT great candidates to aggressively use H.E.A.P.™ and instead are candidates for **Equity Harvesting**.

As you will find out when you read Chapter 6, Equity Harvesting requires you to allocate dollars to a new interest expense that is created when you borrow money from the home to reposition those dollars into a tax-favorable/wealth-building tool. Equity Harvesting reduces the available dollars you would have on a monthly basis, which would make that money unavailable to pay down the debt on the HELOC.

My position is that almost everyone is a candidate either to:

1. NEVER pay off the debt on their home and have maximum debt so that their money can be used to grow in a tax-free manner for retirement purposes; OR,

2. Use H.E.A.P.™ to pay off their home's debt as soon as possible.

The great thing about H.E.A.P.™ is that you can tailor it to meet your needs whatever they may be (so long as you carry a balance in your checking account on a monthly basis).

Readers who use H.E.A.P.™ can use $5,000 withdrawals from the HELOC; or they can set up a first-lien line of credit, or have partial direct deposits...the list goes on and on. Every case will be slightly different; and, while the reduction of the primary mortgage will vary per person, the results will be similar in that the original term of the loan on the primary residence is significantly reduced and thousands of dollars in interest will be saved.

LET'S LOOK AT EXAMPLE 2:

For the following example, let's assume you have the following income and expenses:

-Monthly income (after taxes) = $4,000

-First mortgage balance = **$130,000** (house's fair market value = $160,000)

-Monthly mortgage payment at 6.25% = $800.43

-HELOC interest rate = 7% on a 30-year mortgage

-Total monthly bills (non-mortgage) = $2,000

-Total monthly outlay = **$2,800.43**

What do you do first? Sit down with your H.E.A.P.™ advisor, who will go over your budget and take into account all of the variables in order to create a "real-world," usable budget.

Your H.E.A.P.™ advisor will then take your data and input it into the H.E.A.P.™ software, creating for you a comprehensive, custom three-page report. In that report, among other items, will be the following numbers and chart:

How much was saved in total interest as budgeted using H.E.A.P.™ in Example 2?

Months Paid	Months Saved	Years Paid	Years Saved	Interest Paid	Interest Saved
81	269	6.75	22.42	$28,912	$129,020

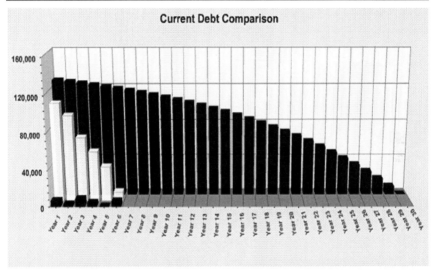

Again, in Example 2, you had a terrific outcome and certainly accomplished your goal of paying off mortgage debt as quickly as possible.

EXAMPLE 3: ASSUMES YOU HAVE HAD A MORTGAGE IN PLACE FOR SEVEN YEARS

So far, my examples are for people who have new 30-year mortgages. That certainly illustrates the power of H.E.A.P.™ at its maximum level, but what if you have had a mortgage in place for, let's say, seven years?

Let's look at the numbers for this 3rd example:

-Monthly income (after taxes) = $6,000 ($72,000)

-First mortgage balance = **$300,000** (house's fair market value = $350,000)

-Monthly mortgage payment at 6.25% = $1,847.15

-HELOC interest rate = 7%

-Total monthly bills (non-mortgage) = $3,000

-Total monthly outlay = **$4,847.15**

In this case, assume that the "**current**" mortgage balance is not $300,000 but instead is $270,100.94 (remember mortgage payments have been made for seven years).

How much was saved in total interest as budgeted using H.E.A.P.™ in Example 3?

Months Paid	Months Saved	Years Paid	Years Saved	Interest Paid	Interest Saved
126	**150**	**10.50**	**12.50**	**$104,308**	**$94,406**

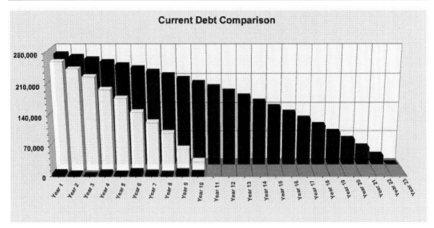

What's interesting to note about this H.E.A.P.™ example is that you have had about the same monthly "surplus" as you did in Examples 1 and 2, but the amount of mortgage interest saved is much less. Additionally, the loan was much larger which might make you think that the savings must be greater.

Remember, in this example, you already had the mortgage in place for seven years. So you've already paid thousands of dollars in interest since the vast majority of each $1,847.15 mortgage payment went to pay interest on the loan. That interest, unfortunately, cannot be saved by using H.E.A.P.™.

Only interest yet to be paid can be saved, and H.E.A.P.™ did a nice job of saving nearly $100,000 in mortgage interest over its remaining life in this example.

EXAMPLE 4:

Let's take a look at another real-world example.

H and W live in a nice new home and maintain a fairly strict budget. Their current mortgage, taken out in November of 2010, is an interest-only mortgage with a $236,000 balance and a $1,202 per month <u>interest-only</u> payment (the full payment amount of $1,700 <u>includes</u> property taxes and homeowners insurance of $498 per month).

They also have a second mortgage with a $39,000 balance and a $300 payment. Their other monthly bills include a car payment, two credit cards, utilities, a gym membership, and insurance. These expenses total $850 per month. Their miscellaneous spending is budgeted to $250 per week and pays for groceries, fuel, and fun. W works part time and H works full time. Together they bring home $1,200 per week after taxes as income.

Creditor	Balance	Monthly Payment
First Mortgage	$236,000	$1,700
Second Mortgage	$39,000	$300
Auto	$11,000	$300
Credit Card	$5,500	$120
Utilities		$200
Gym Membership		$80
Insurance		$150
Groceries, Fuel, & Fun		$1,000
Total Monthly Outlay		$3,850
Total Monthly Income – Take Home (after tax)		$5,200

Currently, at the end of 10 years, the first mortgage will transition from an interest-only mortgage to a fully amortizing mortgage, at which time the payment would increase to $1,724 principal and interest ($2,222 with taxes and insurance), which would equate to approximately a $500 increase.

The following are the steps H and W would need to take in order to implement H.E.A.P.™

Step 1 – Establish a HELOC.

The current second mortgage of $39,000 is a closed-end second mortgage (no draws available). An appraisal verified that the home is currently worth $320,000. A **$60,000** HELOC is established (93% combined loan to value). The interest rate is prime + .25% = 8.5%.

Once the HELOC is established, it would be accessed and used to pay off/replace the current second mortgage of $39,000, leaving them with total monthly expenses of $3,550 [($3,850 current expenses) – $300 (the old second mortgage)]. Therefore, the client would not consider the HELOC debt as part of the normal monthly expenses.

Step 2 – Start the plan. The following chart will show the weekly running balance of the HELOC. The first transaction the client would complete is to access the HELOC to reduce the principal mortgage by $11,000, and the emergency fund is set at $10,000. This creates a new HELOC balance of $50,000 ($39,000 + $11,000).

Date	Transaction	Transaction Amount	HELOC Balance	Available Credit
4/1	Mortgage Reduction	-$11,000.00	$50,000.00	10,000.00
4/6	Payroll	$1,200.00	$48,858.22	11,141.78
4/13	Payroll	$1,200.00	$47,737.87	12,262.13
4/20	Payroll	$1,200.00	$46,617.65	13,382.35
4/27	Payroll	$1,200.00	$45,493.64	14,506.36
5/4	Payroll	$1,200.00		
5/4	Bills	-$3,550.00	$47,917.80	12,082.20
5/11	Payroll	$1,200.00	$46,795.91	13,204.09
5/18	Payroll	$1,200.00	$45,672.19	14,327.81
5/25	Payroll	$1,200.00	$44,546.64	15,453.36
6/1	Payroll	$1,200.00		
6/1	Bills	-$3,550.00	$46,969.26	13,030.74
6/8	Payroll	$1,200.00	$45,845.83	14,154.17
6/15	Payroll	$1,200.00	$44,720.56	15,279.44
6/22	Payroll	$1,200.00	$43,593.46	16,406.54
6/29	Payroll	$1,200.00	$42,464.52	17,535.48
7/6	Payroll	$1,200.00		
7/6	Bills	-$3,550.00	$44,883.74	15,116.25
7/13	Payroll	$1,200.00	$43,756.91	16,243.09
7/20	Payroll	$1,200.00	$42,628.24	17,371.76
7/27	Payroll	$1,200.00	$41,497.73	18,502.27
8/3	Payroll	$1,200.00		
8/3	Bills	-$3,550.00	$43,915.38	16,084.62
8/10	Payroll	$1,200.00	$42,786.97	17,213.03
8/17	Payroll	$1,200.00	$41,656.72	18,343.28
8/24	Payroll	$1,200.00	$40,524.63	19,475.37
8/31	Payroll	$1,200.00	$39,390.69	20,609.31
9/7	Payroll	$1,200.00		
9/7	Bills	-$3,550.00	$41,804.90	18,195.10
9/14	Payroll	$1,200.00	$40,673.05	19,326.95

In five-and-a-half months, the available credit would have increased to nearly $20,000; and a principal reduction of $10,000 could have been made again. The question H and W would have to ask themselves is; do they want to access the line of credit for another $10,000 (and repeat the process to pay down primary mortgage debt) or do they want to continue to pay down the HELOC.

For that matter, H and W would have to decide if they want to access the HELOC at all until such time as they pay down the initial HELOC balance to zero.

Based on the numbers, H and W could pre-pay $20,000 per year on their interest-only first mortgage and pay off the HELOC two times a year so the initial balance of the HELOC does not exceed $39,000 at the end of the year.

Lets' assume they do want to slowly pay down the HELOC to zero. To do that, they will set themselves up to make only one principal reduction per year ($10,000) until the balance of the HELOC reaches $0.00. At that time they could choose to make a $20,000 reduction annually until the primary mortgage is paid off.

After four years, H and W could have paid the HELOC down to zero while also paying down $10,000 a year on their primary mortgage. After the HELOC reaches zero, H and W could then decide whether to access the HELOC for $20,000 and pay that amount down annually on the primary residence until it is paid off or maintain the annual amount at $10,000, which will free up $10,000 for other expenses (for fun, to buy a new car, start funding a college fund, or for any other expense).

Because H & W could choose to go in different directions with this loan, I'll not illustrate the multiple outcomes as you have enough H.E.A.P.™ examples which fully illustrate the power of the program.

THE MILLION-DOLLAR QUESTION: CAN H.E.A.P.™ WORK IF YOU HAVE <u>NO MONTHLY SURPLUS</u>?

This is a great question. What if you spend every dollar you make and no more? In other words, you have no extra money in your checking account at the end of the month. Can H.E.A.P.™ work for you?

You'll be happy to know that it <u>**will work**</u>.

You'll be sad to know that it won't work great or even knock 5+ years off your mortgage; but, so long as it helps to save even a few months of mortgage interest, for 99% of the readers of this book, H.E.A.P.™ is still worth implementing.

The determining factor as to how well H.E.A.P.™ will work if you **DO NOT** have extra money at the end of the month to allocate to pay down your HELOC is your average monthly checking account balance.

Remember that you are using your HELOC as a checking account with H.E.A.P.™; and, as such, you are using "**every available dollar every day**" to pay down mortgage debt. The larger your average monthly checking account balance, the more daily interest you will save.

Let's look at **EXAMPLE 5** in which I will assume that you will have no extra money at the end of each month and you spend every dollar, but no more, of your income each month.

-Monthly income (after taxes) = $ 4,252

-First mortgage balance = **$200,000** (house's fair market value = $250,000)

-Monthly mortgage payment at 6.25% = $1,231.43

-HELOC interest rate = 6.25%

-New 30-year mortgage

-Total monthly bills (non-mortgage) = $3,020.57

-Total monthly outlay = **$4,252**

How much was saved in total interest as budgeted using H.E.A.P.™ in Example 5?

Months Paid	Months Saved	Years Paid	Years Saved	Interest Paid	Interest Saved
342	18	28.50	1.50	$226,267	$17,051

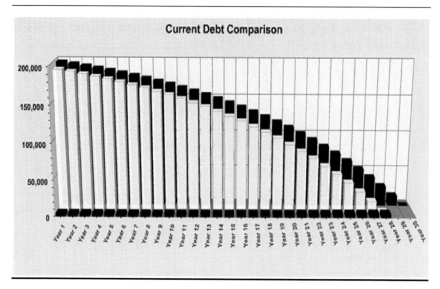

Did H.E.A.P.™ work in this example where there was NO extra money to allocate to pay down the HELOC at the end of the month?

Sure. The savings was $17,051 over the life of the loan.

Is $17,051 worth implementing H.E.A.P.™?

I'll let you answer that for yourself. In my mind, because the cost to set up H.E.A.P.™ is nominal (or even nothing) and because once the plan is set up it really requires very little work, I think a $17,051 savings is worth implementing the plan.

Does Example 5 only apply to those who spend every dollar they earn on monthly <u>bills</u>?

<u>**NO!**</u>

What other kind of reader spends every dollar they make every month but doesn't spend that money only on bills?

It's the reader who is saving money for retirement.

There are many readers of this book who make X amount of money each month and choose to allocate Y amount of that to fund an account for retirement purposes.

For example, many people choose to income-tax defer $1,000-$16,000 a year into a 401(k) plan at work.

Many people choose to fund brokerage accounts with their take-home pay as a way to build wealth.

Many choose to fund 529 plans for their children's or grandchildren's education.

Some people, and a greater percentage of those who've read my **Home Equity Management Guidebook: How to Achieve Maximum Wealth with Maximum Security**, choose to fund a unique wealth-building tool with their take-home pay, where money will grow tax-free and come out tax-free in retirement. (Read Chapter 6 for a summary on Equity Harvesting as a way to build wealth).

Each of these types of people will allocate all or nearly all of the extra money they have left over in their checking account on a monthly basis to build wealth in other ways rather than building wealth by paying down mortgage debt.

If you invest your money in similar ways as these types of people, you would not normally think that H.E.A.P.™ is a plan that can benefit you. However, now that you've seen the real-world math, you know that, even if you do not have extra money left over at the end of the month, you can still use H.E.A.P.™ to save thousands of dollars in mortgage interest.

Remember, there is no risk and no downside to H.E.A.P.™. Therefore, I strongly advocate that you find a local H.E.A.P.™ advisor who can help you properly budget your plan, so you can use "every available dollar every day" to pay down mortgage debt.

To find a local H.E.A.P.™ advisor you can work with, go to www.HEAPlan.com.

DOES H.E.A.P.™ WORK FOR THOSE IN THE LOWER INCOME TAX BRACKETS?

Sure, why not? A dollar saved in interest is a dollar saved. Those who make more money and/or have a larger monthly surplus can benefit more than those who don't make a lot of money or don't have much of a surplus. But the bottom line is that, if you carry a balance in your checking account, you can use H.E.A.P.™

Whenever you can knock off any amount of money from your primary mortgage, you not only pay down the debt but you also stop the compounding of interest on that money. (This is why the previously discussed mortgage acceleration plans—Rounding-Up, Applying the Bonus and Bi-Weekly, knock a few years off the length of a mortgage).

Abnormal Expense Months

Although many people will be able to easily maintain their current spending levels, some people always seem to have a variety of unexpected expenses pop up, such as an appliance breaking, a car repair, or kids begging to go somewhere warm for spring break. Most families will find that a few times per year their "normal" monthly expenses are actually rather abnormal. Christmas is a good example of this.

When the plan is set up, these abnormal months need to be considered. Although an amount needs to be set aside for emergencies, these higher-cost months shouldn't be considered emergencies.

H.E.A.P.™ is very flexible, because the only mandatory payments you need to make are the interest only payments of the HELOC. You can choose to access the HELOC in varying amounts every single year. However, for examples in a book, it works best to assume a systematic plan so that everyone can understand the math and how the plan works.

WHAT ABOUT SERVICING THE HELOC EVERY MONTH?

When I first started talking with people about H.E.A.P.™ and illustrating its power, one of the main questions I would receive is where in the budget do I allocate the cost to pay the interest payment on the new HELOC a borrower will take out when implementing H.E.A.P.™

It's a good question and makes sense. Due to the fact that a borrower has a new loan when H.E.A.P.™ is initially set up (although still the same amount of total mortgage debt on day one), there is a new loan that must be serviced.

Think just for a second what happens with H.E.A.P.™. You set up a HELOC, borrow money from it to be used to pay down the primary mortgage, and then use the HELOC as a checking account. When doing that, borrowers will deposit their paychecks into the HELOC usually twice a month. That is good because it helps a borrower use "**every available dollar every day**" to pay down mortgage debt, but what it also does twice a month is make payments on the HELOC, thereby servicing the HELOC loan. Therefore, no extra payment is needed to service HELOC debt.

My guess is that this explanation will suffice for many as the reason why the borrower does not have to make an additional monthly payment to service the loan. If you have additional questions about how the HELOC is serviced every month, please feel free to e-mail info@HEAPlan.com.

WHAT IF YOU HAVE "OTHER" DEBT (LIKE CREDIT CARD DEBT)?

Many people who want to implement H.E.A.P.™ so they can pay down the debt on their primary residence also have "other" debt.

If you listen to the news, you know that millions of Americans have leveraged themselves not just with debt on a personal residence, but also with thousands of dollars of **credit card debt**. Also, many people have student loans and automobile loans.

Often, the interest rate that is charged on this "other" debt is the same or **higher** than that of a regular mortgage. If that is the case, then such readers should consider using H.E.A.P.™ to pay off that other debt before, or in conjunction with, paying down the debt on the personal residence.

Think about it. If you carry a balance on your credit card, the interest rate is probably in excess of 8% (and, often, over 10%), and the interest on this debt is **NOT tax-deductible**. However, as you read in Chapter 2, Home Equity Debt is tax deductible up to $100,000 of new debt (limited by the FMV of the home).

Therefore, wouldn't it make sense to use a HELOC to pay off credit card debt? Absolutely. By using H.E.A.P.™ with a HELOC, interest on the debt would be tax deductible; and, because you are using H.E.A.P.™, you would systematically pay down the debt on the HELOC much quicker than you would your credit card debt.

The big caveat with credit card debt is to make sure you have the discipline to not run up a bunch of new debt on the credit card after you use the HELOC to pay it off.

Let's consider the following example. Roger and Sherry, married with no children, are in their early thirties. Both have graduated from law school with a substantial amount of student loans and credit card debt that was accumulated during their educations. (I debated whether to put this example in the book as it is a little outrageous, but this is a real-life example of people I know.)

Creditor	Balance	Monthly Payment
US Dept Education	$97,007.00	$311.00
Student Loan MA	$34,793.00	$176.00
Student Loan MA	$28,337.00	$143.00
US Dept Education	$37,000.00	$509.00
Key Student Loan	$13,226.00	$133.00
Key Student Loan	$13,226.00	$133.00
Key Student Loan	$12,686.00	$123.00
CitiCard (cc)	$8,031.00	$321.00
Bank of America (cc)	$7,644.00	$285.00
Chase (cc)	$5,535.00	$211.00
Key Bank (cc)	$5,462.00	$52.00
CitiCard (cc)	$871.00	$67.00
Rooms to Go (cc)	$4,805.00	$109.00
USAA (cc)	$4,354.00	$95.00
GM Mortgage	$97,821.00	$858.00
TOTAL	**$370,798.00**	**$3,526.00**

They purchased a home about two-and-a-half years ago with a small down payment; and, with a little appreciation, they have accumulated about $18,000 of equity in the property.

They both have secure, good-paying jobs; however, their finance charges are not allowing them to reduce their debt.

They have opted to have $1,000 per month from Sherry's paycheck directly deposited into a regular checking account for their utilities and miscellaneous expenses and to have $3,536.50 direct deposited twice a month into a HELOC to be used solely for debt reduction through H.E.A.P.™

Step 1: The Setup

Their current equity allowed them to set up a $15,000 HELOC. Because they have dual incomes, an emergency reserve fund of only $5,000 was established. They also decided to keep the first two credit cards open after they are paid off, which will offer them approximately $10,000 more in emergency reserves. This setup will be maintained until they have built up enough of a cushion to comfortably sustain a potential loss of one income.

A $10,000 withdrawal was made from the HELOC. That money was used to pay off the Chase ($5,535) and Rooms To Go ($4,805) debts (an extra $340 from savings was used to pay off the remaining Rooms to Go balance). This immediately reduced their total monthly payments by $320 to $3,206 ($3,526 was the original total monthly payment to service debts).

The following chart shows the account activity for the first three months:

Date	Transaction	Amount	HELOC Balance	Available HELOC Balance
June 1st	Debt Reduction	-$10,000.00	$10,000.00	$5,000.00
15-Jun	Payroll	$3,536.50	$6,498.43	$8,501.57
1-Jul	Payroll	$3,536.50		
1-Jul	Bills	$3,206.00	$6,190.63	$8,809.37
15-Jul	Payroll	$3,536.50	$2,675.75	$12,324.25
1-Aug	Payroll	$3,536.50		
1-Aug	Bills	$3,206.00	$2,354.60	$12,645.40
15-Aug	Payroll	$3,536.50	-$1,173.68	$16,173.68
16-Aug	Debt Reduction	-$11,173.68	$10,000.00	$5,000.00

On June 1, they eliminated two credit cards using the plan. On August 15, they reduced the debt by another $11,173.68.

As the chart indicates, the clients accessed $10,000 again from the HELOC, as well as the $1,173.68 surplus created by the last direct deposit. The $11,173.68 was used to pay off the CitiCard debt ($8,031) and reduce the Bank of America debt down to $4,501.

This reduced the total monthly payment to service their total debts by $426 a month. Their new total monthly debt service payment dropped to $2,780.

Because their new monthly payments to service debt dropped to $2,780 from the initial $3,526, more money was able to be applied toward paying down the HELOC. This accelerated the pay down of the HELOC, which, in turn, allowed them to pay down their remaining debt quicker.

As you can see in the following chart, Roger and Sherry were able to pay down the $10,000 HELOC by November 1. This allowed the clients to continue with H.E.A.P.™ by accessing $9,232.08 on November 1 ($14,232.08-$5,000, which still left them with their $5,000 emergency fund).

Date	Transaction	Amount	HELOC Balance	Available HELOC Balance
16-Aug	Debt Reduction	$11,173.68	$10,000.00	$5,000.00
1-Sep	Payroll	$3,536.50		
1-Sep	Bills	$2,780.00	$9,278.43	$5,721.57
15-Sep	Payroll	$3,536.50	$5,774.34	$9,225.66
1-Oct	Payroll	$3,536.50		
1-Oct	Bills	$2,780.00	$5,038.01	$9,961.99
15-Oct	Payroll	$3,536.50	$1,519.11	$13,480.89
1-Nov	Payroll	$3,536.50	-$2,012.08	
1-Nov	Bills	$2,780.00	$767.92	$14,232.08

Because of the massive amount of debt, many components were considered when setting up this plan.

For example, the debts with the highest interest rates were the first bills eliminated. Credit card debts usually have the highest interest rates. Student loans typically have lower rates and will follow the credit cards.

The goal is to have everything but the mortgage eliminated within eight years. After that, the mortgage should quickly follow suit.

I understand this is an extreme example, but it is real life; and this example should help you understand how people with a decent amount of "other debt" might choose to use H.E.A.P.™ to pay down non-home mortgage debt.

For people with "other debt," their focus should be the "other debt" that is putting the largest burden on them. They should also realize that significant life changes could occur (children, additional job opportunities, etc.) and eliminating their high-cost "bad" debt first makes better financial sense.

Side Note: Student loans sometimes have very low interest rates. If that is the case for your student loan debt, you need to run the numbers to make sure it makes sense to use the HELOC to pay down that debt.

Variables that will affect this calculation are your income tax bracket, the HELOC rate, the student loan interest rate, and the amortization schedule of the student loans. If you are in a low tax bracket and the interest on the student loans is low, then it would make more sense not to pay off the student loans until after the HELOC and primary home loan balances are paid off.

For auto loans, many sales incentive programs are offering no interest or low interest financing. Again, you need to simply run the numbers based on your tax bracket and interest rates of the auto loan and the HELOC to determine if it makes sense to pay down the auto loan prior to focusing on your home mortgage.

WHEN DOES H.E.A.P NOT WORK AS WELL?

H.E.A.P.™ is less effective in the following circumstances: bruised credit, limited equity, and irregular income.

1) Bruised Credit limits H.E.A.P.™'s effectiveness as it is predicated on obtaining a suitable Home Equity Line Of Credit. These loans sometimes require a higher credit standard than some closed-end mortgage programs. Some lenders will reserve these accounts for people who have managed their credit well. One of the major factors that affect the effectiveness of H.E.A.P.™ is your ability to manage credit; so the two go hand in hand.

Some readers have had bruised credit in the past but have been working very hard to clean it all up. In these cases, simple counseling and determining the direction of how to best repair a reader's credit can help him/her get to the point where the program can be used.

2) Limited Equity also poses a problem for the program. Some people may not have enough available equity to start the program. This may be a result of a recent home purchase with little or no money down. It may also be the result of a recent refinance where cash was obtained to pay off some debt or carry out some home improvements. Or, it could be caused by deflation of the property.

If any of these are the case, one of the other aforementioned acceleration programs could be utilized until your equity position is substantial enough to start H.E.A.P.™. You need to keep a watchful eye on your local housing market for upward trends that may help improve your home's value, which would increase your equity position.

3) Irregular income can also reduce the effectiveness of the program. As you have learned, one feature of the program is that it reduces daily interest charges by utilizing regular deposits directly into a HELOC. This reduction of interest charges helps pay down the debt more rapidly.

Consider a self-employed individual, like a builder, who receives large sums every couple of months. Although the program will still work if this person spends less than he/she makes, interest charges on the money borrowed from the HELOC will accrue for longer periods of time. And if the time between deposits is long enough, there may be situations where the available balance of the HELOC may not be sufficient to support regular monthly payments.

Also, since the HELOC is a loan, if regular payments are not made to service the loan, the lender may limit the borrower's ability to draw more funds from the HELOC until the late payments are made. In cases of irregular income, a more conservative H.E.A.P.™ should be implemented.

For the self-employed individual in the earlier example, using H.E.A.P.™ to force the borrower to allocate more dollars annually to debt reduction still makes sense. When people use H.E.A.P.™, they are more aware of the harmful effects of interest; and, many will **curb frivolous spending habits** because they know every dollar they take out of their HELOC costs them interest every month.

Although these three examples are the most common variables that make the program ineffective or less effective, for certain clients, the program will not make much sense to use.

For example, it makes little senses for a person with a high income or a high net worth to aggressively use the plan. Sure, a wealthy person can use a HELOC to pay off the primary residential mortgage quicker than just making the minimum required mortgage payment each month. However, the question is whether it makes financial sense to do so. In my opinion, the answer is no. Instead, a person with significant financial means should look at Equity Harvesting as a way to build maximum wealth for retirement. (See Chapter 6 for more information).

A FEW THINGS TO WATCH OUT FOR

While H.E.A.P.™ is relatively simple to understand (although not always the easiest to illustrate), there are a few nuances to the plan that you need to watch out for or follow when you implement it.

1) There is more than one kind of "equity line."

Some equity lines are "closed-end" and do not make the unused or paid portion available for withdrawal to the borrower. You access the line once, and then are not allowed to access the remaining balance until the line is paid off. It's basically a one-time draw for a specific amount. This type of loan obviously does not work as you need to use the HELOC as a checking account and access the line of credit every time you write a check to pay your bills (and access large chunks at a time as you pay down your primary mortgage on a periodic basis).

2) The line of credit provided by the institution must be able to accept multiple deposits a month, allow unlimited check writing against the account, and not limit the transactions each month. Hopefully, it also provides some sort of debit card for weekend emergencies.

If your HELOC does not allow for unlimited check writing, you can make one withdrawal a month and transfer enough money from the HELOC to pay your bills from your traditional checking account. This will have very little effect on the finances of H.E.A.P.™, but it is more cumbersome.

3) You need to be able to budget yourself properly and have financial discipline when using H.E.A.P.™ The reason this plans works is because spending habits and miscellaneous spending are budgeted correctly. Although the budget is based on your current spending habits, a stricter budget, if enforced, could speed up the plan even more.

4) You need to keep in mind your ultimate goal. The goal with H.E.A.P.™ is to pay off your primary mortgage as quickly as possible. It is not the best plan to build your wealth, but it is the plan many will choose nonetheless. When you keep this goal in mind and maintain the discipline to stick to it, H.E.A.P.™ will help pay off your home mortgage literally years earlier than you otherwise would be able to.

5) Your "emergency cash fund" needs to be carefully considered.

6) If there is a loss of income and the payments are not made on the HELOC, you need to know whether the bank will allow you to access the remaining line of equity.

Summary of the caveats of the program:

1) You need to have equity in your home.

2) Typical lines of credit are harder to acquire with bruised credit.

3) Local institutions may have limitations on transactions (writing checks), and costs are associated with exceeding the limit.

4) Some lenders may not offer direct deposit.

5) If your home is sold, the equity line would not automatically transfer to the new property. In order to continue the plan on the new home, a new line of credit would need to be obtained and secured by the new property.

6) Many lines of credit have a limited "draw period" or time in which money can freely be taken out. Often, it is as much as ten years. This period should be clearly identified, and a plan should be put in place to pay down the line after the draw period ends. If the plan is maintained, there should always be plenty of available equity; and if scheduled payments are made on time, many institutions will roll the line over into a new one with little or no cost.

WHAT HAPPENS WHEN YOU PAY OFF THE <u>ENTIRE</u> DEBT ON YOUR PROPERTY THROUGH H.E.A.P.™?

There will come a point in the plan at which your mortgage balance reaches $0.00. That will be a happy day for you!

What should you do next?

At this point, you will have proof positive that an entire residential mortgage can be eliminated rather quickly because it was just accomplished through H.E.A.P.™

My hope actually is that many readers of this book who initially implement H.E.A.P.™ will choose to not pay off their mortgage debt.

What did I just say? I hope that those who initially implement H.E.A.P.™ choose not to pay off their mortgage debt.

Why would I say that as the person who created H.E.A.P.™ and who wrote this book to tell readers the virtues of H.E.A.P.™?

The short answer is that, for many, aggressively paying off debt on a home is not the "best" financial decision. For some it will be, but certainly not everyone.

I would rather see many of the readers of this book choose to use Equity Harvesting to build wealth rather than use H.E.A.P.™ to pay down the debt on a home.

Remember, H.E.A.P.™ **isn't for people who want to build the maximum amount of wealth**; it's specifically for people who want to **pay down the debt on their home as quickly as possible** (which does build wealth by reducing overall debt and interest payments but does not build "maximum" wealth).

See Chapter 6 where I have a little summary chapter on how to build "maximum wealth with maximum security" through the concept of Equity Harvesting.

If you do use H.E.A.P.™ to completion where your home's debt is entirely paid off, a decent amount of money will be freed up due to the fact that there are no future mortgage payments to make. At that point, you have several options. You can take the money normally allocated to the mortgage payment and instead use it to:

-party, travel, and play.

-invest in the stock market in a taxable brokerage account.

-tax-defer more income through a qualified plan at work or an IRA.

-fund a low-expense, high cash value life insurance policy (which you can learn more about in my book Retiring Without Risk (www.retiringwithoutrisk.com)).

Realistically, many borrowers do not choose to reposition or invest a lot of their extra dollars. It doesn't seem to be the American way. We are a consumption society, always looking to buy that next toy, take that next trip, and buy that bigger house.

For those interested in how to use H.E.A.P.™ in a little different way to start building more wealth rather than paying off the home's debt as quickly as possible, please turn to Chapters 6 & 7 where I will show you just how to do so.

HOW CAN YOU RECEIVE SPECIFIC NUMBERS TO DETERMINE IF AND HOW H.E.A.P.™ WILL WORK FOR YOU?

Great question. I imagine many readers of this book will want to know how H.E.A.P.™ will work to pay off their home's debt. I don't blame you.

As this topic becomes more popular, you will find advisors trying to sell you this concept and **$3,500** software packages so you can implement it yourself (which you can read more about in Chapter 5 where I discuss the "Bad" mortgage acceleration plans).

Fundamentally, with this book, my goal is to educate you with real-world math on home equity management topics so you can be informed and make the best decisions for yourself.

Having said that, the best way to determine if H.E.A.P.™ is a good plan for you is to work with an advisor who has the H.E.A.P.™ software and can properly illustrate how the plan will work with your particular situation.

If you do not know a local advisor who can help you with H.E.A.P.™, please feel free to go to www.HEAPlan.com and sign up for a consultation; and an advisor near you will contact you.

Also, if you have a local advisors you know and you want them to get up to speed on the proper way to budget and help clients with H.E.A.P.™, feel free to send them to www.HEAPlan.com where they can sign up to learn more.

H.E.A.P.™ SUMMARY

As with anything in life, a game plan is only as good as the follow through. Certainly, most homeowners, if asked, would say they'd like to pay their home off early. Homeowners who want to pay off the debt on their home as soon as possible should jump at the opportunity to use H.E.A.P.™ due to the fact that the program can accelerate mortgage pay off by several years, thereby saving thousands, and sometimes hundreds of thousands, of dollars in interest payments.

Many homeowners are already using the common debt reduction plans like Rounding Up, Applying the Bonus, and/or Bi-Weekly Payments. While there is nothing wrong with these plans, H.E.A.P.™ is a much better program in many ways.

H.E.A.P.™ is a flexible plan that can adjust when you need the plan adjusted. The key to the plan is to always pay down maximum debt as you have your income/paycheck directly deposited into your HELOC where the surplus in the account will automatically be applied to pay down mortgage debt at the end of each month.

If you use H.E.A.P.™ and have the discipline to stick with the program, you will pay off your home early. There is no doubt about it.

Let me go back to my initial statement when I started this chapter:

> Is it a fair statement to say that there are two types of people in this world? There are those who want to use the equity in their homes to tax-favorably build a retirement nest egg, and there are those that want to pay off the debt on their home as soon as possible.

I believe the answer to the above statement to be yes; and, hopefully, after reading this entire book, you will determine whether you want to **pay off your home mortgage debt early** using H.E.A.P.™ or whether you need to investigate using the equity in your home to build "**Maximum Wealth with Maximum Security**."

Chapter 5
"Bad" and "Ugly" Mortgage Acceleration Plans To Stay Away From

If you've read my other mortgage industry standard book, **The Home Equity Management Guidebook: How to Achieve Maximum Wealth with Maximum Security** (www.thehomeequitymanagementguidebook.com) or my book **Bad Advisors: How to Identify Them; How to Avoid Them** (www.badadvisors.com), you already know I pride myself in not only helping readers understand the "**right**" way to implement certain wealth-building concepts but also telling readers, with clarity, the "**wrong**" way to implement such plans.

If you have not yet read my other books, I need to help you understand why I go out of my way to make sure you also learn the "**wrong**" way to implement the plans discussed in my books (and others). Here are three reasons:

1) 99% of the books in the marketplace that tout themselves as "the" way to build wealth or pay off debt early are pitching you a specific strategy that the authors hope you will implement. Many authors are not trying to educate you on all sides of the topic or point out the pitfalls as well as the potential benefits of what they are discussing. I think it's fair to say that it is not in an author's best interest to tell you the downside to the topics they are discussing because doing so would hinder sales of their books and whatever else the author is trying to sell you.

So, while you may learn some things from these books, you usually only receive half of the story. This can be devastating to you financially if you blindly follow the author's advice.

2) Most people who read wealth management books like my Home Equity Management Guidebook are either somewhat or totally unfamiliar with the topics discussed. Like most readers, you are probably reading books in order to learn more. This, of course, leaves you vulnerable to misinformation. Because you are not completely familiar with the "best" ways to build wealth pitched in "get-rich-quick" books (or, in this case a "pay-off-your-debt-early" book), you do not yet have the baseline knowledge of the concepts

discussed to be able to **question the author** and the validity of his/her methods to build wealth or eliminate debt.

Again, this can be very dangerous to your wealth if you blindly follow the advice in these books, causing you unnecessary expenses or even great financial tragedy.

3) Without a complete education on the topics discussed in "get-rich-quick" books or "become-debt-free" books, you are susceptible to salespeople (the author as well as other advisors) who use the books to sell you on the concepts discussed.

So what? Who cares?

You should, as there is a cottage industry of financial planners, mortgage brokers, insurance agents, and other advisors who use for-public books to push the sales of life and annuity products and/or mortgages and, yes, become-debt-free programs in a manner that is **NOT** in your best interest. They do so because of the perceived credibility of a "published" author in hopes that the book will bolster their credibility and the sales concept they'd like to sell to readers to whom they give the book.

Consider the following scenario:

Assume your "trusted" financial planner, mortgage broker, CPA, etc., sent you a book in the mail that is supposed to show you how you can build a large, tax-favorable retirement nest egg. The book is supposed to reveal the "secrets" that only the "wealthy" know; and, if you read the book and implement the strategies discussed, you will be able to "become a millionaire" without work or risk (which, by the way, doesn't exist).

Assume you eagerly read the book as you certainly want to learn how to become a millionaire without work and without risk.

Assume that after you completed this easy-reading book, you determined that you, in fact, would like to implement some of the strategies discussed NOW so you could start your journey to become a millionaire.

Who are you going to call to help you on this journey? Of course, you are going to call the advisor who gave you the book, right? (Because obviously that advisor must know how to help you with the strategies discussed in the book) Bingo!

This marketing strategy worked exactly as the advisor had hoped; and in the process of helping you become a millionaire, the advisor himself/herself becomes a millionaire by making large commissions off of the products that were recommended in the book and sold to you, the unsuspecting reader.

Finally, I want you to assume that the plan didn't quite work out as you planned; and for reasons you don't understand (and were not discussed in the book), you don't seem to be on your way to becoming a millionaire.

Actually, after two to three years into your journey to become a millionaire, you are feeling a bit duped and start researching the Internet to see if you can find anyone else who has been sold a bill of goods based on the book you read that got you started on this journey.

After surfing the Internet for only a few minutes, you happened upon a website that was specifically created to point out the problems with the book you read, the sales pitch that goes along with the book, and the pitfalls that can befall readers who take the author's word at face value.

While reading this website, your face turns beet red. You come to the conclusion that you have been sold a plan that was not going to make you a millionaire as planned and could potentially cause you significant financial heartache.

IF the author would have been <u>intellectually honest</u> with readers and given the pitfalls of the concepts, many readers would never implement the concepts because they are not good candidates for the plan(s) in the first place. However, that doesn't sell books or help advisors push products. Unfortunately, in the marketplace today, there are many books and sales programs that DO NOT give the downside to the financial concepts they teach.

If you think the story above is one I just made up as fiction for this book, it isn't. There really are such books in the marketplace; and, if you want to learn about two books I recommend you stay away from, go to www.www-MissedFortune101.com and www.www-StopSittingOnYourAssets.com.

These addresses may look like they have a typo in them because there is a second set of www's in them, but that is exactly how you want to type the addresses into an Internet web browser. The second set of www's stands for **W**hat's **W**rong **W**ith. I think you'll find the websites entertaining as well as educational. They will drive home the reason that it is important in books like this one and my <u>Home Equity Management Guidebook</u> to tell both the pros and cons of the strategies discussed.

How does all of this apply to H.E.A.P™ and other mortgage acceleration plans in the marketplace?

Good question.

I hope I've done a good job in this book explaining H.E.A.P.™ and exactly why it can work to help you pay down your mortgage and other debt years sooner. I meant what I said in that H.E.A.P.™, if implemented and budgeted correctly, has no downside and no risk (which sounds contrary to my initial comments in this chapter which are that get-rich-quick plans and mortgage acceleration plans do have a downside that you need to know about).

This chapter isn't so much about what's wrong with H.E.A.P.™ if implemented correctly because I stand by my statements that there is no risk and downside when you properly set up H.E.A.P.™. This is a vital chapter to help you **stay away from** what I call the "Bad" and "Ugly" mortgage acceleration plans that you may run into in the marketplace.

"BAD" MORTGAGE ACCELERATION PLANS

What I'm about to say is going to make me sound like I'm talking in circles or talking out of both sides of my mouth, but hang in there with me. After a short explanation, you'll understand exactly where I'm going and why this could be the most important chapter of this book.

The "Bad" mortgage acceleration plans I'll be discussing work in a manner virtually identical to the way H.E.A.P.™ does to pay down mortgage debt.

Confused?

How can a mortgage acceleration plan that works virtually identical to H.E.A.P.™ be "Bad"?

Good question.

The fundamentals of H.E.A.P.™ are what they are. If you recall from the core chapter where I explained exactly how H.E.A.P.™ works, you'll see that in its basic form H.E.A.P.™ works by using a HELOC as your checking account.

You set up a HELOC, access it in an amount that makes sense for you ($5,000, $10,000, $15,000), and apply that money towards your primary mortgage. Then you use the HELOC as your primary checking account. This allows you to use **"every available dollar every day"** to pay down mortgage debt; and at the end of every month, your "surplus" will be applied to the HELOC, which over time will pay down to zero. When your HELOC reaches zero, you access it again in the appropriate amount, pay down your primary mortgage again, and continue to use the HELOC as your checking account.

While the plan is fairly simple on its face, I indicated that the best way to go about implementing H.E.A.P.™ is to **work with a certified advisor** who has the needed expertise and software to be able to put together a client-specific plan with proper budgeting.

Let's get back to the question, "How can a mortgage acceleration that works just like H.E.A.P.™ be "Bad"?"

The answer is simple, and I think you'll agree with me.

How much should you pay an advisor to help you with H.E.A.P.™?

Think about this for a minute. The advisor is going to spend time with you to understand your finances, use a sophisticated software program that specifically helps properly budget you to implement a plan correctly, and holds your hand to actually follow through with implementation. The typical advisor is going to spend 2-4 hours of his/her time to help you. What's that worth to have a properly setup and budgeted plan?

My opinion is that while it's definitely valuable, you should be charged $500 or less.

That seems more than reasonable to me as H.E.A.P.™ will save many readers in excess of $100,000 in mortgage interest on a new mortgage. I'll let you make the determination for yourself.

$3,500 MORTGAGE ACCELERATION PLANS

What if the advisor wanted to charge you **$3,500** to help you set up H.E.A.P.™?

(By the way, I can guarantee that will never happen with H.E.A.P.™ because if I hear of an advisor charging more than $500 for their time to help someone set up H.E.A.P.™, I will take their password away to the web-based H.E.A.P.™ software they need to help you set up a plan. I will also post their name and contact information on a special part of my **www.badadvisors.com** web site where I tell visitors the "Bad" advisors I recommend they stay away from).

Getting back to the question, "Would you pay **$3,500** to learn how to pay off your mortgage 5-10-15+ years early with a plan that will save you $50,000-$100,000+ in mortgage expenses over the life of your loan?"

Your initial answer after reading this book should be an emphatic NO.

Why?

Because you know that H.E.A.P.™ exists with advisors who, by agreement, CANNOT charge you more than $500 to help you set up and implement a plan.

Let's assume you didn't know this book existed or that H.E.A.P.™ existed.

Be honest with yourself. If a trusted advisor of yours (CPA, financial planner, mortgage broker, etc.) came to you with a H.E.A.P.™-like plan where they illustrated that you could pay off your mortgage 10+ years early and save over $100,000 and indicated that the cost to set up the plan was **$3,500**, would you pay the money and implement the plan?

Because I've had calls and/or e-mails from hundreds of consumers who were pitched the **$3,500** program, I know that many readers said yes or were seriously considering spending **$3,500** to implement a H.E.A.P.™-type plan. (I say "were" because, after a person learns about H.E.A.P.™, they typically refuse to pay **$3,500** for what is essentially the same program).

If you said to yourself that you're not sure, would it help if I told you the company selling you the **$3,500** program would be happy to finance the **$3,500** fee? Would that help you make the decision? (How nice of them to add to your debt so you can pay their **$3,500** fee.)

"MAGIC" SOFTWARE

Let me change the sales pitch of the **$3,500** program. What if the sales pitch went something like this:

Advisor: Mr. Smith, I'm going to show you a life-altering plan that will help you get out of debt 5-10-15 years early and save you over $100,000 of mortgage interest on your home loan.

Mr. Smith: Really? That sounds great. I'm all ears.

Advisor: Ok, here's how the plan works. The first thing you need to do is buy the magic/unique/groundbreaking software package that has recently been created. This software is one of a kind, and it will guide you on a daily basis to pay off your mortgage early.

Mr. Smith: Wow! That must be some software program.

Let me stop here and point out the obvious **difference** between the sales pitch for the "Bad" **$3,500** mortgage acceleration program and H.E.A.P.™.

What is different about the sales pitch? A **$3,500** software package.

Hmm. Does that make much sense to you?

It should **NOT,** since you've just read this book where I've told you how H.E.A.P.™ works; and you didn't hear me say anything about needing "magic" software to make the program work.

I did say that it's important to work with a "trusted" advisor who had software to properly budget and help you set up H.E.A.P.™; but you have not heard me discuss the fact that you, as a consumer, actually need special or "magic" software to make H.E.A.P.™ work.

Now I'd like you to forget you've ever heard of H.E.A.P.™ or been educated on how these types of mortgage acceleration plans work. I know it's not easy to do, but play along with me; and the point I'm making about "Bad" mortgage acceleration plans will become crystal clear.

Let me ask you a few questions.

-Aren't we in an age where "technology" is doing things for the average consumer we never thought could be possible?

Sure.

Who ever thought we'd be able to have flat screen/plasma TVs, satellite radio, iPods, iPhones, Blackberry's, wireless Internet, and all of the wonderful technology in the medical fields which is truly mind blowing.

We are getting so used to new technology rolling out and making our lives easier and better that we don't even get surprised anymore when new technology hits the street in a reasonably economical and usable manner for the average consumer.

Therefore, when an advisor knocks on your door and says he/she has "magic" software that can help you pay down your mortgage years earlier and save you $100,000+ in mortgage interest, doesn't that sales pitch make sense?

I can guarantee you it does; because as I've already stated, many unsuspecting consumers have purchased the **$3,500** program with "magic" software.

We all know there is a price for technology, right? The more unique and sophisticated, the better it is; the more it makes our life easier or can save us money, the more it's going to cost, right? That's "supply and demand" in our country. If one company came out with "magic" software that could save a consumer $100,000+ on mortgage interest, could the company selling the software charge a pretty penny for this software? Sure.

Let's get back to our discussion/sales presentation with the advisor and Mr. Smith.

Advisor: Yes, Mr. Smith, this new software is really special and unique and a real bargain at **$3,500**.

Mr. Smith: A bargain? Well, I'm not sure it's a bargain; but I must say that I would very much like to pay off my mortgage early and save $100,000+ in mortgage interest in the process. Can you tell me more about this program?

Advisor: Mr. Smith, I happen to have an illustration with me based on our earlier discussion about your income and expenses; and, sure enough, if you use this "magic" software, you will pay off your mortgage in 8.5 years and save $133,000 in mortgage interest over the life of the plan.

Mr. Smith (with mouth wide open and eyes popping out of his head while looking at the illustration): WOW! What else can you tell me about this software and how this plan works?

Then the advisor explains to Mr. Smith exactly how the plan works, which sounds an awful lot like how H.E.A.P.™ works except it is based on the premise that the program works **because of the software**. Let's pick up the sales pitch after the advisor finishes explaining, in essence, how a H.E.A.P.™-type plan works to pay off a mortgage early (except with the tie in with the "magic" software).

Advisor: Mr. Smith, so do you understand how this "magic" software works to help you use every available dollar every day to pay off mortgage debt?

Mr. Smith: Well, I sort of understand that. Let me see if I have it correct: 1) I have to buy this software to make the program work; 2) I have to obtain a HELOC, access it, and take the borrowed funds and pay down my primary mortgage with that money; and 3) then I use the HELOC as my checking account. Is that about it?

Advisor: Yes, Mr. Smith, it seems as though you understand it pretty well. I'd like to tell you some other benefits to our "magic" software.

Mr. Smith: Do tell.

Advisor: Once you buy the **$3,500** software package, you get tech support from our team; and if you have any questions about how to run the software, you can call that team. Also, the software is transferable in that you can take it with you if you buy a new house and have a new mortgage. Also, because I know you are concerned about the **$3,500** fee, I wanted you to know that the company selling it will finance that $3,500 so you don't have to come out of pocket to purchase the software and implement the plan.

Mr. Smith: That sounds good.

Advisor: Mr. Smith, what do you think? Are you ready to sign up and spend $3,500 on this one-of-a-kind "magic" software program/mortgage acceleration plan?

Mr. Smith: Can you let me sleep on it? I like the sound of your program and "magic" software, but I'm not sure about this **$3,500** fee......

What do you think of the sales pitch this advisor gave to Mr. Smith?

If you've read Chapter 4 of this book, I hope your opinion is that there is something **very wrong** with this sales pitch.

What's the main problem with the sales pitch I just went over?

YOU DO NOT NEED "MAGIC" OR OTHER SOFTWARE TO IMPLEMENT A H.E.A.P.™-TYPE MORTGAGE ACCELERATION PLAN.

I'd say that's a fairly significant problem, wouldn't you?

Let me elaborate on the "magic" software used in the **$3,500** mortgage acceleration plan.

First, I'd like to state that the "magic" software is really cool. I'll give this company their due. The software is what I call "dynamic" in that it is supposed to be a daily valuation software. What does that mean? Once you start using the software, IF you want to spend the time (and many won't) to input on a daily basis, your expenses paid and income deposited into your HELOC account, it's supposed give you a daily picture of how long it will take to pay off your mortgage and how much interest you'll save.

That is neat, isn't it? Sure it is.

Is it "**$3,500** neat" for purchasers of this software to see every day or even every month how their income and expenses affect the ultimate payoff date of their loan and how much interest they will save?

Let me put that another way. If you could implement a plan like H.E.A.P.™ where you paid an advisor $500 to set up your mortgage acceleration plan with proper budgeting and the plan would pay off your mortgage in essentially the same amount of time as the plan where you had to spend **$3,500** for "magic" software, which one would you rather buy?

Keep in mind that, no matter what the software says today when telling you how much money you will save and how quickly you will pay off your mortgage, once your plan is set up, the software is **not** really helping you pay down your mortgage quicker. It's simply telling you how you are doing on a daily basis (and only after you spend the time to input all the numbers manually into the software).

If you didn't answer that you would rather use a H.E.A.P.™ -type plan because it works essentially the same way without allocating **$3,500** for neat software (but one that really has NO "magic,"), I must have done a terrible job explaining to you how H.E.A.P.™ works. If you didn't come to that conclusion, I strongly recommend you re-read Chapter 4 so you can see how simple H.E.A.P.™ is and why you do not need "magic" software to make the program work.

Keep in mind that H.E.A.P.™, once set up, **runs itself**. After you take out your HELOC to pay down your primary mortgage, you simply use the HELOC account as your checking account and live your life as you normally do. No "magic" software can help you spend less money or make you more money (both of which are the two ways you can further accelerate your mortgage payoff date).

What if you are curious to know if you are still on target to pay off your mortgage early through H.E.A.P.™? I have three simple answers for that:

1) Call your H.E.A.P.™ advisor and ask him/her to re-run your numbers based on your now lower mortgage debt, your HELOC debt, and your current income and expenses. Your information will be saved in the advisor's H.E.A.P.™ software, and it should take him/her a few minutes to re-run numbers for you.

If your advisor is hard to get in touch with or can't find the time to help you in timely manner, call me. I'll run the numbers for you myself (and then call the H.E.A.P.™-trained advisor to see why he/she is not giving you good service).

2) Spend **$3,500** on "magic" software that doesn't help you pay down your mortgage quicker than a program without "magic" software, but will give you a daily status of how you are doing with paying off your mortgage debt.

Hopefully 2) doesn't make you scratch your head too much. Am I actually advocating that you spend **$3,500** on the "magic" software that has no magic? Not really. I'm simply stating that, if it's important enough for you to know what your daily balances are on your mortgage acceleration plan even though the software doesn't help you pay down your mortgage any quicker than a plan that doesn't use "magic" software and you understand this fact, then I don't have a problem with you buying the software. I think it's a terrible financial decision, but we all have free will in this country.

3) Actually, there is no need for me to even state 2) in this part of the book. If you really want your own software, I do sell my H.E.A.P.™ software to non-advisors for a one-time fee of $100 (money that is donated to the H.E.A.P.™ Charitable Foundation).

MLM SALES PLATFORMS

I'm not sure if the term MLM means much to you or not. Some readers of this book will see the term MLM and chills will go up their spine. Why? Let me first tell you what MLM stands for if you don't already know. MLM stands for **Multi-Level-Marketing**.

Most people who know what MLM means do not think too kindly of items being marketed with the platform.

Let's try to look at this from a little different angle. Have you ever heard of a pyramid scheme? Most people have. A pure pyramid scheme is illegal. Why? It's a scam.

I actually ran into one in college once. I had a suite-mate in the dorm come over to my room and tell me he ran into a get-rich-quick scheme. Being a poor college student, I was all ears. He said he was in a pyramid plan where he was going to make X thousands of dollars. I was very curious and asked him how the plan worked.

He said that he bought into the plan by spending $500. I said that was a bit steep, and he said it was nothing compared to what he was going to make. I said, "Do tell." He said that his chore was to find five other people who would pay $500 to buy into the pyramid, and he wanted me to be one of them. I said that I didn't follow him. He said that, when you recruit people and they find people to pay the fee, I would make X amount of money when each one of the recruits paid the fee.

But it was better than that. When the people that I recruited recruited others who recruited others, I would make a commission (to use a crude term) on each person in my "down line."

For example: If I recruit five of my own people to spend $500, I will earn, let's say, $200 from each one. Three-hundred dollars of the $500 each of my recruits would pay would go "up line." So my suite-mate would make, let's say, $200 on my $500 fee and $150 on each of my recruits.

Then when my five recruits found their five people to pay $500 to get into the pyramid, I would make $150 on each of their recruits (that number being 25 x $150 because I had five recruits who recruited five of their own recruits). Also, my suite-mate would make $100 on my recruits' recruits (25 x $100).

So, after one level of the pyramid, I make my $1,000 (five recruits paying $500 of which I kept $200 for a total of $1,000). Therefore, after one level, I'm making money.

When my recruits find five of their own recruits to pay $500, I would make $150 x 25 = $3,750.

When those 25 recruits recruited 25 people, let's say I would make $100 on each one of them (25 x 25 = 625 x $100 = $6,250)

My total revenue after three levels of the pyramid would be $11,000 for my initial $500 investment.

To many, including my dad, Roccy, Sr., it sounded crazy (and is illegal). Therefore, after much thought and counsel from Sr., I took a pass on the MLM/pyramid scheme that was pitched to me back in college (and, by the way, some pure pyramid schemes work and people can make a lot of money—even though they are illegal).

Let's get back to the **$3,500** H.E.A.P.™ -type mortgage acceleration program. There is a **$3,500** H.E.A.P.™-"type" mortgage acceleration plan in the marketplace with "magic" software that has a quasi-MLM income model for advisors who get involved to sell it.

How would such a plan work? It's fairly simple. Someone starts this "magic" software company and then goes to recruit agents in the field to sell it. From the **$3,500** fee, the agents make X amount of "commission" when they make a sale to the consumer, and the rest goes to the company issuing the software.

Then, if the first level of agents "recruit" a team of their own advisors to sell this same **$3,500** program, the agent will earn an override-type fee when sales are ultimately made to the consumer.

I want you to know that in the real world the **$3,500** quasi-MLM "magic" software mortgage acceleration plans exist. The recruiting that is going on is unlike any I've ever seen. The plan is being pitched to mortgage brokers, life insurance agents, financial planners, real estate agents, property and casualty insurance agents, and even to the most trusted advisor, the CPA.

Many of the above-mentioned advisors are also going out and recruiting non-financial and non-mortgage professionals to sell the plan. This is a bit laughable because I can guarantee you that the vast majority of "professional" advisors do not understand what they are selling so the chances that a non-professional understands what they are selling is slim to none.

How can that be?

H.E.A.P.™ and H.E.A.P.™-"type" plans are simple, right? You just learned the basics by reading this book and know that you can work with a H.E.A.P.™ advisor who cannot by agreement charge more than $500 to properly budget and implement your plan.

INTENTIONAL OR UNINTENTIAL MISLEADING

Since I created H.E.A.P.™, I've been contacted by literally thousands of advisors. I have three types of advisors who contact me to learn more about H.E.A.P.™:

1) Advisors who learn of H.E.A.P.™ from my e-newsletters, other books, or from articles I have published in trade journals.

These types of advisors are interested in learning about H.E.A.P.™ for themselves and to help their clients. They are not aware of "other" acceleration programs in the marketplace.

2) Advisors who have seen other mortgage acceleration plans (including the "Ugly" one I'll be discussing shortly) and happened across H.E.A.P.™ in their research.

These types of advisors sort of understand why H.E.A.P.™ and other similar plans work and seem genuinely interested in seeking out the best plan for themselves and their clients.

3) Advisors who have already signed up to sell the "Bad" plan (and maybe, unfortunately, sold a few) or are seriously considering selling the "Bad" plan.

I have hundreds of conversations with advisors who signed up to sell a "Bad" **$3,500** mortgage acceleration plan. The conversation goes something like this:

Advisor: Roccy, I came across your H.E.A.P.™ plan, and I want to know how it differs from the **$3,500** mortgage acceleration plan. I signed up (or I'm thinking of signing up) to sell this plan, and the **$3,500** fee is rubbing me the wrong way.

Roccy: You don't say? I'd be happy to tell you why H.E.A.P.™ is different and why I consider it the ONLY client-first/client-friendly program in the marketplace.

Then I explain to the advisor basically what you've already read in this chapter.

-There is no such thing as "magic" software to help you pay down a home mortgage.

-That the **$3,500** "magic" software mortgage acceleration plan, as I've been told by dozens of advisors who are contracted to sell it, is the most misleading sale in the financial services/mortgage industry today.

-That advisors selling the **$3,500** program are either ignorant or are intentionally and purposely misleading their clients in order to make the sale.

-That H.E.A.P.™ works essentially the same way to help clients pay down their mortgage; but the maximum fee an advisor is allowed to charge for his/her advice is $500 (although advisors are permitted to give clients a discount at their discretion).

Then the discussion usually goes as follows:

Advisor: Are you saying that if I sell the **$3,500** plan I am misleading my clients?

Roccy: Essentially, yes! Answer the following questions for me: Does the software itself help the client pay down their mortgage quicker than the mortgage acceleration plans that do not use this "magic" software?

Advisor: Not really.

Roccy: Do you disclose to the client that the software **DOES NOT** really help them pay down the mortgage quicker?

Advisor: No.

Roccy: Then you have confirmed to me that the sale is absolutely misleading. An honest sales pitch will tell the client that, with proper budgeting, they can receive what effectively is the same result with H.E.A.P.™ or even other mortgage acceleration plans that do not use "magic" software.

Advisor: I've been told that, if the client does not pay something significant for their Mortgage Acceleration Plan, they will not use it.

Roccy: This is total nonsense. Similar mortgage acceleration plans have been around for nearly 20 years and have worked just fine without software. H.E.A.P.™ does not charge the client for "magic" software, and it works just fine.

Advisor: O.K., but if a client doesn't input their daily expenses into the plan, they won't know when their HELOC needs to be re-accessed and won't "utilize" the program correctly.

Roccy: Again, total nonsense. What you are giving me sounds like talking points from a sales presentation which helps advisors lie to themselves and justify the **$3,500** fee so they can give the same sales pitch to their clients.

What you should know is that I've had several calls from advisors who've sold a **$3,500** program to clients and they have told me that the clients figure out in about three to four months that the "magic" software doesn't do anything. Then clients get upset with the advisor for selling it to them and stop using it. While clients stop using the "magic" software, they continue using their HELOC to pay down their mortgage (as they would have if they used H.E.A.P.™ from the start). What you need to understand about H.E.A.P.™ is that, once it is properly budgeted and setup, the plan runs itself without any "magic" software.

Basically, clients finally figure out what they purchased was a **$3,500** alarm clock that will tell them when their HELOC balance is getting near zero and that it needs to be re-accessed so the primary mortgage can be paid down again.

Anyone who can read their monthly HELOC statement can tell for himself that the HELOC needs to be re-accessed because it is nearing zero (and some banks have HELOC balances online).

My guess is you now fully understand why I'm so upset with the sale of "magic" software for **$3,500**.

My point to advisors is that, if you always do what's right for your clients, you'll be in the industry a long time and will make a good living on your normal services.

Don't try to make a living selling **$3,500** "magic" software that has no magic and will harm your reputation locally.

Unfortunately, many advisors selling "magic" **$3,500** software packages are doing so to supplement their normal income because they are not doing well with how they currently make a living.

Actually, I've heard from many of the advisors who have contacted me that this is part of the sales pitch. I've been told that advisors are told that the sale of the software is so powerful and they can make so much money selling it that they should consider making it their primary income instead of their current way of making a living (mortgages, financial services, insurance, etc.).

In my opinion, this is a recipe for disaster, as eventually the entire country will know that the **$3,500** software package has no "magic", and this will ruin the reputation of advisors selling it.

SUMMARY ON THE "BAD" MORTGAGE ACCELERATION PLANS

I suppose I can sum this up in a few words: If you are being pitched a **$3,500** "magic" mortgage acceleration plan, run for the hills. Tell the advisor you are very familiar with it (more so probably than the advisor selling it), and then tell the advisor to do some research and find a mortgage acceleration plan they can sell that is "client-first" vs. "advisor-first" (and point them to www.HEAPlan.com if you want).

H.E.A.P.™ will get you to the same place as any of the other mortgage acceleration plans in the marketplace. And when you work with a H.E.A.P.™ advisor, you will know that you are working with one who has your best interest as his main objective rather than churning clients to purchase expensive software they don't need.

HOW DOES THE "UGLY" MORTGAGE ACCELERATION PLAN WORK?

At this point, you should be a quasi-mortgage acceleration plan expert. While you may not have the H.E.A.P.™ software to properly budget yourself, you should fully understand how H.E.A.P.™ and other similar plans work to pay down a mortgage. (And so far you know that it's not because of **$3,500** "magic" software).

If you are waiting for me to explain how the "Ugly" acceleration plan works differently than the **$3,500** "Bad" plan or H.E.A.P.™, you can stop waiting because the "Ugly" plan works off the same principles, with one difference.

Let me just go through the sales pitch of the "Ugly" acceleration plan, and I think you'll understand why I call it "Ugly."

Advisor: Client, it's your lucky day. I'm going to show you how to pay off your mortgage 5-10-15+ years early with a mortgage acceleration plan that can be implemented without changing your lifestyle. I'm going to show you how to use "**every available dollar every day**" to pay down mortgage debt. The program probably will save you over $100,000 in mortgage interest over the life of the loan.

Mr. Smith: That sounds great. I'm all ears.

Then the advisor explains to Mr. Smith exactly how the plan works which sounds an awful lot like how H.E.A.P.™ works except it is based off the premise that the client must use a **"special" type of mortgage** to make it work.

The main difference with the "Ugly" acceleration plan is that the client does NOT need to obtain a $5,000-$10,000 HELOC that in H.E.A.P.™ is accessed and used to pay down the primary mortgage. Why, and if not, then how can the plan work?

The "Ugly" acceleration plan IS a HELOC. There is no need to obtain another HELOC as the client's **entire mortgage is moved to a 1ˢᵗ position HELOC,** which is then used as the client's primary checking account.

From a pay-down-your-mortgage-quicker standpoint, it works the same as H.E.A.P.™. Clients will deposit their paychecks into the HELOC account, which will allow them to use "**every available dollar every day**" to pay down mortgage debt. If clients have a surplus in what would have been a checking account at the end of any given month, that amount will be applied automatically to pay down the mortgage principal.

So far it should sound a lot like H.E.A.P.™, and it might even sound simpler due to the fact that that you do not need to go through the step of accessing a separate HELOC every time you want to make a payment towards the primary mortgage.

Let's pick up the sales pitch after the advisor finishes explaining, in essence, how a H.E.A.P.™-type plan works to pay off a mortgage early (except with the tie in of a "special" mortgage program).

Advisor: Ok, now that you understand the basics of how this mortgage acceleration plan works, what do you think of the illustration I just gave you where you will pay off your mortgage 20 years early and save $135,000 in mortgage interest?

Mr. Smith: It's very powerful. I like it. What do I need to do to implement this program?

Advisor: It's really quite simple. I need you to **refinance** your current mortgage into the unique 1st position HELOC mortgage, and you'll be all set and ready to go.

Mr. Smith: That's it? What's the catch?

Advisor: Catch? Oh, did I tell you that the mortgage interest rate floats monthly?

Mr. Smith: Floats? What do you mean? It's not a 30-year fixed mortgage?

Advisor: No. The interest rate is tied to LIBOR + typically a 2.5% margin and literally can change up or down monthly. The loan is, however, "amortized" over 30 years.

Mr. Smith: Isn't that risky? And what's a margin?

Advisor: No, that's not risky. Look at how LIBOR has been so low over the last several years. As for a margin, that is the additional interest that is added to the one month LIBOR rate. So if LIBOR is 4.5% this month, your rate would be 7.5%.

Also, I wanted to let you know that you can "buy down" the rate.

Mr. Smith: What do you mean "buy down" the rate?

Advisor: For 1-2% of the total amount of the mortgage (due at closing), you can literally buy down the rate by 1-2% points. Therefore, in my example, if your fully indexed rate is 7.5%, you could buy it down to, let's say, 6.5%.

Mr. Smith, let's get back to that illustration I ran for you. Let's keep our eyes on the ball. This unique program is going to save you $100,000+ in mortgage interest. If that's the case, it surely can't be too expensive or risky.

Mr. Smith: I suppose. So what you are saying is that I **"have to"** refinance in order to take advantage of a mortgage acceleration program?

Advisor: **Yes**.

Before I tell you what's wrong with the "Ugly" mortgage acceleration plan, let me point out why this sales pitch can be categorized as dishonest (intentionally or not).

It was that last question Mr. Smith asked. He asked if he "had to" refinance his entire mortgage into a 1st position HELOC in order to take advantage of a mortgage acceleration plan. The answer was yes which is absolutely **FALSE**. You now know that since you know how H.E.A.P.™ works.

Now let's illustrate the main problem (besides the misleading sales pitch) with the "Ugly" mortgage acceleration plan. It's really quite simple if you have not already figured it out.

H.E.A.P.™ or a H.E.A.P.™-type mortgage acceleration plan only requires that you be able to recycle typically a $5,000-$15,000 HELOC.

There is NO need and NO requirement that you refinance your ENTIRE mortgage into a 1st position HELOC to make the program work.

If the "Ugly" plan is so bad, then why does it still illustrate where a person can pay off his or her mortgage 5-10-15+ years early, thereby saving the average person $100,000 worth of mortgage interest?

Fundamentally, the "Ugly" plan is the same as H.E.A.P.™. It works the same exact way EXCEPT it requires the client to trade in their current mortgage (which, for most, is a fairly low 30-year fixed rate) for what can be a very expensive monthly floating interest rate, which during most lending environments will have a significantly higher interest rate.

Buying down the interest rate is nonsense as that can be done with any mortgage; and, therefore, there is no advantage with doing so with the "Ugly" acceleration plan.

Because the "Ugly" plan works for the exact same reasons as H.E.A.P.™ works, it will illustrate very powerfully for a potential buyer of the plan. It's still using "**every available dollar every day**" to pay down mortgage debt. It's still applying the surplus at the end of a month to pay down mortgage debt.

However, if you compared a H.E.A.P.™ illustration to an "Ugly" illustration, H.E.A.P.™ will help a client pay down the mortgage quicker because the primary mortgage rate a client has in most lending environments will be less.

It's just that simple.

In addition, H.E.A.P.™ is a **safe program** because you are allowed to keep your current secure and low interest rate loan for a majority of the debt on your home.

WHY DO CONSUMERS BUY INTO AND USE THE "UGLY" MORTGAGE ACCELERATION PLAN?

Again, the answer is simple. If a person is pitched the "Ugly" plan and has no other plan to compare it to, it's going to illustrate very powerfully; and the consumer is going to be counseled that they MUST refinance in order to take advantage of the program.

Most consumers (no matter how smart) are going to see the power of the plan; and, because they do not know the questions to ask to poke holes in the sales pitch and are unaware of other alternatives, they will be motivated to move forward with this risky and unnecessary mortgage acceleration plan.

HOW DOES AN ADVISOR MAKE MONEY WITH THE "UGLY" MORTGAGE ACCELERATION PLAN?

Think about it for a second. You were counseled to move your current mortgage (which could be $100,000-$500,000+) into a new, very expensive mortgage in order to take advantage of the plan.

The advisor is making significant money on the mortgage sale (much more than **$3,500** in most cases) which is why many greedy mortgage brokers sell this mortgage program over the "Bad" plan and certainly over H.E.A.P.™.

I imagine many of you are wondering why an advisor, from a selfish standpoint, would want to help clients with H.E.A.P.™. The maximum an advisor can charge for advice to budget and set up a plan is $500. They can't make any money doing that, can they? That hardly covers the time spent helping the client.

Believe it or not, and contrary to the impression I may have given you in this book, there are many "client-first" advisors in this country–not nearly as many as there should be, but they are out there, and they are gravitating towards H.E.A.P.™.

Advisors using H.E.A.P.™ to help clients are not non-profit advisors. They are using H.E.A.P.™ as a reason to start a dialogue to give potential new clients a reason to sit down and talk with them.

They are using H.E.A.P.™ as a value-added service for existing clients.

Generally speaking, advisors using H.E.A.P.™ are confident enough in the services they normally provide and their professionalism that they believe that once clients have interaction with them on H.E.A.P.™ they will want to learn more about the normal or usual services these advisors have to offer.

That sort of sounds like a bait and switch. Get someone in the door on one topic and pitch them another.

Not at all.

110

A classic bait and switch is where someone is pitching something that sounds like it has a value and then turns out not to and was used to get someone in the door so other products/concepts could be sold.

H.E.A.P.™ can benefit any client who has a primary mortgage, and that benefit can be in excess of $100,000 of mortgage interest savings. So there is no bait and switch going on with H.E.A.P.™ .

In my opinion (which I suppose is tainted since I created H.E.A.P.™ and regulate who can use it), if you are working with an advisor for the first time and that happens to be because of H.E.A.P.™, you are lucky that you found one of the few "client-first" advisors out there. I suggest and hope you learn about the other services that the advisor has to offer so they can help you.

You know what's funny about mortgage acceleration plans?

Think of the following:

-If you talk with an advisor pitching the "magic" software "Bad" **$3,500** mortgage acceleration plan, you'll be told that you MUST use their software in order to make the plan work.

-If you talk with an advisor pitching the "Ugly" mortgage acceleration plan, you'll be told that you MUST refinance your entire mortgage into a 1st position HELOC in order to make a mortgage acceleration plan work.

You now know that the sales pitch by both types of advisors is NOT accurate.

You now know that the advisors pitching these plans are either totally ignorant of the proper way to help a client pay down their mortgage quicker with a "mortgage acceleration plan", or they do know and have chosen to intentionally mislead clients with either the "Bad" or "Ugly" plans in the marketplace (which make the advisors significantly more money on the sale of the programs).

So which do you prefer? An advisor who is incompetent or unethical?

With a H.E.A.P.™ advisor, you should avoid both.

SUMMARY ON THE "BAD" AND "UGLY" MORTGAGE ACCELERATION PLANS

Because I've made this chapter longer than I anticipated, let me keep the summary short and to the point.

There is NO need to use what I call the "Bad" and "Ugly" mortgage acceleration plans.

When being pitched these plans, you are either dealing with an undereducated advisor or an advisor who is fully educated and has chosen to bring you a plan that is in their best interest instead of yours. If that is the case, I recommend telling the advisor to move on to peddle their plans on other, more unsuspecting clients/pigeons.

With H.E.A.P.™, you can work with a "client-first" advisor who will help you set up the only "client-friendly" mortgage acceleration plan in the marketplace.

Actually, once you have found a knowledgeable advisor who understands all of the proper "Home Equity Mortgage" techniques, don't be surprised if you are told that paying off debt on your home is NOT the best way to accomplish your financial and estate planning goals.

For more information on the other side of the Home Equity Acceleration Plan and to learn more about how to build "Maximum Wealth with Maximum Security," you can purchase my book, **The Home Equity Management Guidebook** (**www.thehomeequitymanagementguidebook.com**).

Virtually all advisors who are familiar with H.E.A.P.™ will also be familiar with what's in my **Home Equity Management Guidebook** and can properly counsel you on how to implement H.E.A.P.™ or how to leverage your home's value to grow the maximum amount of tax-favorable wealth.

Finally, if you want to determine whether any of the advisors you are currently are using are "good or "bad," go to **www.badadvisors.com**.

Chapter 6
<u>Equity Harvesting (EH)</u>

I know you bought this book in order to learn the best way to pay off your mortgage 5, 10, 15+ years early, without changing your lifestyle, through H.E.A.P.™. But in good conscience, I could not keep from you a potentially life-changing wealth building strategy that is the opposite of H.E.A.P.™. This strategy is called Equity Harvesting.

Remember that H.E.A.P.™ is a program designed to help you pay off your mortgage early; it is **NOT** designed to help you grow your wealth at a maximum rate and more specifically **NOT** to create a tax-favorable retirement nest egg.

This chapter is meant to round out your education of "Home Equity Management" vs. just teaching you how to pay off a mortgage early.

So, while the vast majority of this book is about getting rid of debt as quick as possible, this particular chapter will explain to you why **<u>DEBT IS GOOD</u>** and how you can use debt to build "<u>Maximum Wealth with Maximum Security</u>."

As you read this chapter, remember that there are only two types of people in this world. There are those that want to use the equity in their homes to build a tax-favorably retirement nest egg, and there are those who want to pay off the debt on their home as soon as possible.

No one wants to simply pay down a home mortgage over 30-years, which maximizes the amount of money lenders are making (which is not in anyone's best interest except the bank).

DEFINING EQUITY HARVESTING (EH)

I define Equity Harvesting as follows:

EH is removing equity from a personal residence or commercial property through refinancing (or a home equity loan) where the borrowed money is repositioned into cash value life insurance.

Equity Harvesting is done for two main reasons:

1) To build wealth in a tax-favorable manner.

2) To asset protect the equity of the home or commercial property.

Reason number 1) is the main reason most people use Equity Harvesting; and, as a nice bi-product (when set up correctly), you can also asset protect your home's equity (as no creditor is going to want a home riddled with debt).

Equity Harvesting can also be defined in the context of **selling a home**. This is actually more tax beneficial because home acquisition debt can be written off on most clients' tax returns, whereas home equity debt typically cannot be written off when the borrowed money is repositioned directly into a cash value life insurance policy with the contemplation of borrowing from it. I'll explain more about this later.

After money is removed from the home, it needs to be repositioned somewhere to help you grow your wealth, preferably in a tax-favorable manner.

THE TOOL OF CHOICE

The tool of choice to help you build your tax-favorable retirement nest egg is **cash value life insurance**.

In my book; The Home Equity Management Guidebook: How to Achieve Maximum Wealth with Maximum Security (**www.thehomeequitymanagmentguidebook.com**), I literally go into chapter and verse everything you need to know about Equity Harvesting to build wealth.

I also cover in great detail how to build wealth in a tax favorable manner in my book Retiring Without Risk (**www.retiringwithoutrisk.com**).

I don't want to allocate 50+ pages on using cash value life insurance as a retirement tool so I'm going to ask that you take my word (for now) on some issues I don't have the space to discuss in this book.

The main concept I'd like you to assume to be true and functional in the real world is that you really can grow "maximum wealth with maximum security" using the "proper" cash value life insurance.

Why and how?

In both my Retiring Without Risk book and Home Equity Management Guidebook, I detail specifically with real-world, verifiable math just how cash value life can work to build wealth. For this book, I'll simply state that the reason people use cash value life insurance as a wealth building tool is because, once funded, cash in the policy **grows tax-free** and can be **removed tax-free** in retirement.

Some people liken cash value life insurance to an unlimited Roth IRA.

I recommend a unique kind of life insurance policy called Equity Indexed Universal Life Insurance (EIUL). (Also known as "Retirement Life™" life).

Why?

Let me ask you a few questions.

If you could build wealth with a tool that would allow you to partake in the upswings of the stock market with a cap of **15%** but with **principal protection** so that in any given year when the stock market goes down **you do not have market risk**, would that interest you?

It should. Money that is actively in the stock market can go up by 15% or more in any given year but can also go down 15% or more in any given year.

Building wealth is not always about what you can return when the market does well; it is also about avoiding negative returns (like the nearly -50% downturn in the market from 2000-2002 and nearly -60% downturn from the highs of 2007 to the lows of 2009).

Would you like a wealth-building tool where after it is funded you will not pay dividend or capital gains taxes on the growth or income taxes on the money when removed? That's a no-brainer—"Yes".

A good EIUL policy will protect your money from downturns in the stock market, provide upside growth potential that tracks the market (with an annual cap of 15%), and allows money to grow and be removed entirely tax-free.

I'm sure many readers will still be skeptical, so let me ask you the following question.

What have you averaged as a rate of return over the last 25-years on your investments?

Would it interest you to know that the cash in an EIUL policy that has the aspects of the one I just described would have returned on average **9.13% over the last 25 years** (with <u>NO risk of loss due to market downturns</u>).

Hopefully I have your attention now so I can move on to illustrate the power of Equity Harvesting as a wealth building tool.

FUNDAMENTALLY, EQUITY HARVESTING IS SIMPLE

There is nothing overly complicated about Equity Harvesting.

To implement an Equity Harvesting plan to build your wealth, you simply 1) borrow equity from your home and 2) reposition that money into a low-expense, overfunded, cash-building, non-MEC life insurance policy.

The cash in the life insurance policy grows without tax and can be removed tax-free in retirement.

That's it. Wasn't that simple?

If that was really all you needed to know, my <u>Home Equity Management Guidebook</u> and my Retiring Without Risk book would only be a handful of pages instead of in excess of 200. So while the fundamentals are really that simple, you need the details on how to do it properly. This chapter will provide you an overview; but if you are serious about Equity Harvesting, you will want to get the books to guide you.

WHO IS A GOOD CANDIDATE FOR EQUITY HARVESTING?

<u>First,</u> in order to be a candidate for Equity Harvesting, you need to have equity in your home. Obviously, the more equity you have in your home, the more you can take advantage of the concept.

<u>Second,</u> it helps if you have decent credit. Why? Because most readers will implement an Equity Harvesting plan by removing equity from their current house, and that will require a new loan. In order to obtain that new mortgage, you will have to have adequate credit.

<u>Third,</u> you or your spouse needs to be healthy. Why? Because when you implement Equity Harvesting correctly you will reposition the borrowed funds into a cash value life insurance policy. If you are not healthy, buying cash value life insurance to build wealth will be cost prohibitive.

The above three requirements are really the main ones you absolutely have to have in order to use Equity Harvesting to build your wealth in a tax-favorable manner.

CAUTION

The concept of Equity Harvesting is one of the most abused in the financial services/insurance industry. With sales books in the marketplace that use "fuzzy" math and ignore the tax code, planners are running around touting these books and making sales of plans to clients who have no business being in them.

To read about the books with "fuzzy" math that you'll want to stay away from, go to **www.www-MissedFortune101.com** and **www.www-StopSittingOnYourAssets.com**.

Therefore, before you run out and implement an Equity Harvesting plan, think about the following qualifying questions:

1) Do you have a stable income?

2) Do you have a stable marriage?

3) Do you have other wealth besides the equity in your home?

4) Are you in a profession where disability is possibility?

5) Are you over the age of 60?

Questions one through four above reveal a high financial risk factor which could affect your ability to financially follow through with the proper funding of an Equity Harvesting plan. Not following through can have devastating financial affects.

Question five is an issue because the older you are, the more difficult it is to make Equity Harvesting work due to the cost of insurance.

It's important for you to make sure you are a candidate for Equity Harvesting before jumping in with both feet to build wealth through such a plan. Notwithstanding the fact that pure marketers of this topic will tell you there is "no risk" and that you are an ignorant fool for not using this powerful tool to build your wealth, Equity Harvesting is NOT for everyone.

EQUITY HARVESTING

Simply put, for many readers, Equity Harvesting will be one of the single best ways for you to build your wealth for retirement.

Wow, that's a bold statement, and one which needs to be quantified.

What do I mean by the "best" way to build wealth for retirement? When I say best, I mean that the concept has the following characteristics:

-Implementing a plan will have **little or no effect on how you currently live your lifestyle** (meaning, after you implement an Equity Harvesting plan, you do not have to forego eating out for dinner, buying gifts for loved ones, or taking vacations).

-**The plan's "risk" factor is very low**. If you reposition money into the "**right**" cash value life insurance policy, the risk of you being hurt financially with an Equity Harvesting plan is very low. With the "**right**" policy, you will have a minimum guaranteed rate of return on the cash in your policy as it grows tax-free; and the returns will be pegged to the best stock index, the S&P 500.

118

-**The wealth that can be created using the equity in your home is significant**. Those who implement an Equity Harvesting plan will significantly increase their overall wealth rather than simply pay down the debt on a home that appreciates. (Remember, a home appreciates whether it has debt on it or not). I will illustrate how much wealth in the next several pages.

ILLUSTRATIONS

I can pontificate for pages about how wonderful Equity Harvesting is from a financial standpoint and that would be interesting reading to some, but I'd rather just get right to the numbers so you can see for yourself how powerful the concept of Equity Harvesting can be to grow your wealth in a safe environment.

The best way to understand the benefits of Equity Harvesting is to use examples.

Example

This will be the everyday middle class American example (Mr. Smith). My "Joe lunchbox" example will be for a married couple who have a home with a fair market value (FMV) today of $235,000.

I know there are many statistics out there which state that the "average home value" is higher, but I believe those numbers are skewed by the many mega-homes that are being built these days.

Mr. Smith is 45 years old, has 2 children, a spouse who works and, generally speaking, has no idea how to save money for retirement. The "breadwinner" earns $50,000 a year, and the other spouse earns $28,000 a year. The couple has all the normal expenses that anyone else has, with a few extra dollars every year that they try, and then never end up, putting away for retirement.

Mr. Smith's home was purchased for $185,000 seven years ago and that the current debt on the home is $135,000 (I assumed the house has appreciated at a conservative rate of less than 4% annually). Mr. Smith put 20% down on the house when purchasing it, and over time he has also paid down some of the debt on the house.

Assume the loan on the home is currently at 6.5% with a 30-year mortgage payment of $935 a month.

I will assume Mr. Smith has good credit (which is a pre-qualifier to being able to use the program).

IMPLEMENTING EQUITY HARVESTING

While Mr. Smith could remove 100% of his equity, I will assume he will harvest the equity through a home equity line of credit (not a refinance) and will remove an amount that will bring his overall loan balance to 90% debt on the property. Therefore, Mr. Smith could remove **$76,500** of equity ($235,000 x 90% = $211,500; $211,500-$135,000 = $76,500).

Mr. Smith will then reposition the removed equity into an EIUL insurance policy where the cash will grow tax-free and be removed tax-free in retirement. Mr. Smith should pay premiums into the cash-building policy over a five-seven year period so as to minimize the death benefit and maximize the cash value.

I will assume Mr. Smith will borrow $15,300 every year from his home equity line of credit for five years and reposition that money into a cash value life insurance policy.

HOW MUCH COULD MR. SMITH REMOVE "TAX-FREE" FROM THE POLICY IN RETIREMENT?

For simplicity, I will assume with all of my retirement examples that Mr. Smith will withdraw money from ages 66-90 (25 years).

I will also assume that the life insurance policy has a return of 7.5% annually as growth on the cash value in the policy (a conservative number for the equity markets).

The amount Mr. Smith could borrow **tax-free** from his life insurance policy is **$23,000 each year for 25 years** for a total amount of **$575,000**.

$23,000? You probably thought I would show you some huge number for as much as I built up the concept of Equity Harvesting.

Understand that Equity Harvesting is one tool to help you build wealth. For this example, Mr. Smith only harvested $76,500 of equity; and in retirement he received tax-free $575,000. That's not bad at all.

The real kicker is: What would Mr. Smith have done if he did not implement an Equity Harvesting plan? You know the answer to this question. They would have **done nothing**. Therefore, $23,000 a year is a significant improvement to Mr. Smith's retirement income.

What is the cost to Mr. Smith for having an interest-only loan on $76,500 of equity?

If the home equity line of credit is at 7.5%, the costs to Mr. Smith would be $478 a month or $5,737 a year.

Therefore, when trying to create an apples-to-apples comparison between Mr. Smith using an Equity Harvesting plan and doing nothing, Mr. Smith needs to invest $5,737 every year into the stock market and let it grow. Then I will compare how much money he could remove from that account from ages 66-90 to how much could be removed from this cash value life insurance policy.

Really, this is not a real-world example due to the fact that Mr. Smith is probably **not** going to invest the $5,737 every year if he didn't implement an Equity Harvesting plan. Most Mr. Smiths of the world would figure out a way to spend/waste the money. In this book, I will give Mr. Smith the benefit of the doubt so I can run comparison examples.

For these examples, I'll assume a 20% blended tax rate (capital gains/dividend tax which is very conservative). I'll assume 50% of the average annual mutual fund expense (50% of 1.2% is .6%) and 50% of the average money management fee (50% of 1% = .5%).

In my opinion, the numbers I am using are very conservative. I use conservative numbers to show you that, even when money grows in the stock market with fewer expenses than are typical, Equity Harvesting works better as a tool to grow your wealth.

For these examples, I assumed the money would grow at a gross rate of 7.5% annually (the same rate as the funds will grow in the life policy).

If Mr. Smith invested $5,737 every year in the stock market, he could remove **$19,038** a year every year after-tax from his brokerage account from ages 66-90.

Remember how much Mr. Smith could remove from his cash value life insurance after-tax? **$23,000** every year from ages 66-90.

How much <u>better</u> did Mr. Smith do by using <u>Equity Harvesting</u> to build wealth vs. <u>doing nothing</u> and simply investing money after-tax in the stock market?

$3,962 a year or $99,050 over the entire withdrawal period.

Wait, you say, this is not a fair comparison because there is still $76,500 of debt on the home? That is true and can be factored into the equation a few different ways. Two of them are as follows:

1) Mr. Smith has a $114,399 death benefit that will pay income-tax free from the life insurance policy if he were to die at age 90. That will more than pay off the $76,500 debt on the home.

If Mr. Smith pays off the debt on the home from the death benefit, his after-tax retirement income **increased by more than 20%** using Equity Harvesting vs. the do-nothing scenario.

2) Mr. Smith could choose to pay down the debt on the house using just over the last three year's of loans from the policy and he still comes out on top. Option 1) is more preferable and more likely to happen.

CHANGING THE VARIABLES

My previous numbers for the EIUL insurance policy were very conservative. What if I made them more real world? By real world, I mean that I will assume a small spread between the lending rate on the life insurance policy loans and the crediting rate on the cash inside the policy.

These are called <u>variable loans</u>, and I do not have time to fully explain them in this book. If you'd like a detailed discussion of how variable loans work in life insurance policies, you can buy <u>The Home Equity Management Guidebook</u> (**www.thehomeequitymanagmentguidebook.com)** or <u>Retiring Without Risk</u> (**www.retiringwithoutrisk.com**); or you can e-mail **info@HEAPlan.com** and I'll forward you a brief PDF summary explanation.

With a small loan spread, Mr. Smith would be able to remove tax-free from his life insurance policy **$26,800** every year from 66-90. This would be **$5,691** a year better or **$149,025** better over the withdrawal period compared to post-tax investing.

See the following numbers from the actual life insurance illustration. (I've taken several years out of the chart to make the size more manageable.)

Age	Premium Payment	Cash S. Value	Death Benefit	Tax-Free Loans
45	15,300	8,075	331,589	0
46	15,300	20,102	331,589	0
47	15,300	36,700	331,589	0
48	15,300	54,445	331,589	0
49	15,300	73,422	331,589	0
55	0	108,726	331,589	0
60	0	156,418	331,589	0
65	0	227,838	331,589	0
66	0	217,643	303,047	26,800
70	0	175,811	226,558	26,800
75	0	121,979	147,336	26,800
80	0	72,781	110,930	26,800
85	0	37,170	94,436	26,800
90	0	28,896	114,379	26,800
95	0	270,379	296,111	0
100	0	738,311	777,245	0

You'll notice that in these illustrations I did not use a high cash value life insurance policy (another subject I don't have space to discuss in this book). I assumed Mr. Smith is financially stable and doesn't need to use one.

What if the interest rate on the life insurance policy loan is consistent with where interest rates have been and crediting rates have been over the last 20+ years?

Mr. Smith would be able to remove tax-free from his life insurance policy **$30,000** every year from 66-90. This would be **$9,161** a year better or **$229,025** better over the withdrawal period as compared to post-tax investing.

See the following numbers from the actual life insurance illustration. (I've taken several years out to make the chart size manageable.)

Age	Premium Payment	Cash S. Value	Death Benefit	Tax-Free Loans
45	15,300	8,075	331,589	0
46	15,300	20,102	331,589	0
47	15,300	36,700	331,589	0
48	15,300	54,445	331,589	0
49	15,300	73,422	331,589	0
55	0	108,726	331,589	0
60	0	156,418	331,589	0
65	0	227,838	331,589	0
66	0	214,535	299,939	30,000
70	0	161,677	212,425	30,000
75	0	99,632	124,989	30,000
80	0	53,754	91,903	30,000
85	0	41,739	99,005	30,000
90	0	90,689	176,172	30,000
95	0	457,241	482,973	0
100	0	1,127,901	1,166,834	0

The previous numbers prompt me to remind you of the positive aspects of the proper cash value life insurance policy.

One of them is that there are annual principal guarantees inside an indexed equity life universal insurance policy, and the gains on the growth each year are locked in.

With money actively traded in the stock market, there is **NO principal protection**; and as nearly everyone found out between 2000-2002 and again between 2007-2009, the market not only goes backwards, but it can do so swiftly and dramatically.

One of the others is the ability to use or not use the **variable loan feature**. Many actuaries believe that over the long term the interest rate on loans in policies will lag crediting rates of the S&P 500 by more than 2%. This is an option which can significantly increase the amount of money you can borrow from a life insurance policy WITHOUT increasing the actual rate of return on the cash in the policy. This is NOT possible with a brokerage account.

One last positive aspect to remind you of is the fact that, from day one of funding the life insurance policy, Mr. Smith had a $331,000 death benefit. Therefore, if Mr. Smith died early, his beneficiaries would receive much more money than if he had simply invested money into a typical brokerage account.

DO NOTHING

Let's re-examine how much better Mr. Smith did by using Equity Harvesting vs. doing nothing. In the "real world," doing nothing means spending every penny you have and not saving.

In this chapter and my examples, I want you to assume that doing nothing means allocating the money Mr. Smith would have used to pay interest on a loan and instead using that money to fund a brokerage account to build wealth.

Then I will compare how much money can be removed from the brokerage account to how much money can be removed from his Equity Harvesting plan (which was funded using a cash value life insurance policy).

The following is a summary chart listing the previous numbers. The numbers below <u>Loan 1</u> come from the life insurance illustration where I assumed <u>NO spread</u> between the interest rate on the loan and what the S&P 500 credits in the policy.

<u>Loan 2</u> is with a <u>1% spread</u> on the borrowing rate (meaning the lending rate on the loan is 1% less than what the S&P 500 will credit in the policy). <u>Loan 3</u> is with a 2% spread on the borrowing rate.

	After-Tax From Brokerage Account	Tax-Free Loan 1	Tax-Free Loan 2	Tax-Free Loan 3
From ages 66-90	$19,038	$23,000	$26,800	$30,000
Total for 25 years	$475,950	$575,000	$670,000	$750,000
Improvement with EH		$95,000	$194,050	$274,050
% Improvement with EH		20%	41%	58%

SUMMARY OF THE FIRST MR. SMITH EXAMPLE

The previous chart should really crystallize the benefits of Equity Harvesting. With very conservative assumptions, Equity Harvesting improved Mr. Smith's cash flow by 20% in retirement. With a 1% spread on the borrowing rate, cash flow improved by 41%; and with Loan 3 (which is what most "experts" think will happen), Mr. Smith's cash flow improved by 58%.

<u>That's the power of Equity Harvesting</u>.

Also remember that the equity indexed life insurance policy Mr. Smith used is a conservative wealth-building tool due to the fact that the policy has an annual growth guarantee and locks in upside gains annually (something you would never be able to do with money invested in the stock market).

Mr. Smith also had a nice death benefit to protect the family; and if the past 20+ years is any indicator of the future, he should end up with over $100,000 more in tax-free dollars from his Equity Harvesting plan than simply funding a brokerage account.

ARE YOU SOLD ON EQUITY HARVESTING AS A WAY TO BUILD WEALTH?

That's not really my goal with this chapter (especially since this is a book on H.E.A.P.™, which shows you how to pay off debt on home, not leverage it to grow more wealth).

I'd say that the previous example makes a very compelling argument for why readers should use Equity Harvesting to build wealth.

WHAT ABOUT THE HOME MORTGAGE INTEREST DEDUCTION?

The interesting thing about the previous example is that it worked even though Mr. Smith did **NOT** write off the interest on his home equity debt. (IRS Title 26 Section163 limit on writing off a refinance or home equity loan is limited to $100,000 of new debt and 264(a)3 prevents the deduction altogether if the borrowed funds are moved into a cash value life insurance policy).

I have an entire chapter on The Laws That Govern Equity Harvesting in my Home Equity Management Guidebook. For this chapter, what you need to know is that some people can be postured to take advantage of the interest deduction through exceptions to 264(a)3 and some can't.

Obviously, if you can write off the interest on the loan, the plan becomes much more economically viable.

Now let's assume that Mr. Smith **CAN** use one of the ways to posture his $76,500 of home equity debt as tax deductible.

How will writing off the interest on the loan affect the financial viability of Equity Harvesting (which you know from what you have already read works well even if you do not write off the interest on the loan)?

You'll recall that with the Mr. Smith example I had him remove $76,500 of equity from the home with an interest rate on the loan of 7.5%. That created a new interest payment for him of $5,737 annually.

In the previous examples, I assumed for comparison that Mr. Smith invested the entire $5,737 into the stock market earning 7.5% annually as a gross investment return.

Now I will illustrate the numbers for Mr. Smith assuming he **can** write off the interest on the $76,500 of home equity debt.

Because readers will be in several different tax brackets, I'm going to show you the numbers for the 15%, 30% and 40% tax brackets. I am also assuming that Mr. Smith itemizes his deductions on his tax return.

If Mr. Smith is in the 15% income tax bracket, he would get a $5,737 deduction on his taxes when he pays the interest expense on the $76,500 loan. The "real" cost to Mr. Smith is not $5,737 but instead is **$4,876**. Therefore, when I create the financial comparison between Equity Harvesting using life insurance and doing nothing and investing money in the stock market, I will allow $4,876 to grow instead of $5,737.

If Mr. Smith is in the 30% income tax bracket, his real cost to borrow the money annually would be **$4,015**.

If Mr. Smith is in the 40% income tax bracket, his real cost to borrow the money annually would be **$3,442**.

Let's see how much money Mr. Smith could take out of a brokerage account after-tax from age 66-90 in the three different tax brackets.

In the 15% income tax bracket, he could remove $16,181 yearly from ages 66-90 for a total of $404,525.

In the 30% income tax bracket, he could remove $13,324 yearly from ages 66-90 for a total of $333,100

In the 40% income tax bracket, he could remove $11,442 yearly from ages 66-90 for a total of $286,050.

Let's see how Equity Harvesting using life insurance with the numbers from earlier examples compares to post-tax investing in the market with the money Mr. Smith would have had to allocate to the interest expense.

128

The following chart is eye-popping. For the chart, I used only the **most conservative** numbers when Mr. Smith accesses tax-free loans from his life insurance policy.

	Brokerage Acct. (15%)	Brokerage Acct. (30%)	Brokerage Acct. (40%)
From ages 66-90	$16,181	$13,324	$11,442
Total for 25 years	$404,525	$333,100	$286,050
	L.I. Policy	L.I. Policy	L.I. Policy
From ages 66-90	$23,000	$23,000	$23,000
Total for 25 years	$575,000	$575,000	$575,000
Improvement with EH	**$170,475**	**$241,900**	**$288,950**
% Improvement with EH	**42%**	**73%**	**101%**

Because of the power of variable loans, I wanted to show you the numbers when there is a 1% spread in the lending rate vs. the borrowing rate and when there is the predicted 2% spread.

With a 1% spread, Mr. Smith could borrow $26,800 each year from ages 66-90 for a total of $670,000.

	Brokerage Acct. (15%)	Brokerage Acct. (30%)	Brokerage Acct. (40%)
From ages 66-90	$16,181	$13,324	$11,442
Total for 25 years	$404,525	$333,100	$286,050
	L.I. Policy	L.I. Policy	L.I. Policy
From ages 66-90	$26,800	$26,800	$26,800
Total for 25 years	$670,000	$670,000	$670,000
Improvement with EH	**$265,475**	**$336,900**	**$383,950**
% Improvement with EH	**66%**	**101%**	**134%**

With a 2% spread, Mr. Smith could borrow $30,000 each year from ages 66-90 for a total of $750,000.

	Brokerage Acct. (15%)	Brokerage Acct. (30%)	Brokerage Acct. (40%)
From ages 66-90	$16,181	$13,324	$11,442
Total for 25 years	$404,525	$333,100	$286,050
	L.I. Policy	L.I. Policy	L.I. Policy
From ages 66-90	$30,000	$30,000	$30,000
Total for 25 years	$750,000	$750,000	$750,000
Improvement with EH	**$345,475**	**$416,900**	**$463,950**
% Improvement with EH	**85%**	**125%**	**162%**

To say that Equity Harvesting works better if you can write off the interest would be an understatement.

When I tell clients and advisors that Equity Harvesting is nearly a no-brainer from a financial standpoint if you can write off the interest, now you know why. The numbers also make a great argument for why Equity Harvesting is close to a no-brainer even if you can't write off the interest.

SUMMARY ON EQUITY HARVESTING

I put this chapter in the H.E.A.P.™ book because the fact of the matter is that many people who think they are good candidates to build wealth through paying off their mortgage through H.E.A.P.™ are really much better candidates to build wealth through an Equity Harvesting plan.

Simply put, Equity Harvesting can be one of, if not, the best way for many readers to build a tax-favorable retirement nest egg. While Equity Harvesting is not a cure-all method to fix the shortfall of retirement wealth that nearly every reader has, the concept has many more pros than cons.

I know I only touched on the surface of Equity Harvesting in this chapter, but my goal was to pique the interest of those who may be candidates so that they can ask their H.E.A.P.™ advisors for information not only on H.E.A.P.™ but also on Equity Harvesting.

As I've stated a few times in this book, if you had an advisor who was nice enough to give you this book to read or one who simply recommended it, it is likely that the advisor is familiar with the topics covered in the book and can run illustrations for your particular situation to determine if an Equity Harvesting plan makes sense for you.

Finally, be very careful with this concept as there are many advisors pitching it who are basing their advice on the books in the marketplace that use "fuzzy" math and ignore the tax code. Working with the wrong advisor on an Equity Harvesting plan can cause you financial ruin.

If you can't find an advisor you feel comfortable with, please feel free to contact me with questions or for a referral to an advisor who has attended my training on this subject matter by going to **www.thehomeequitymanagmentguidebook.com** and requesting more info. I'll help you connect with an advisor who can help you implement a plan that is in your best interest and is done in an honest, safe, and legal manner.

Chapter 7
Using H.E.A.P.™ to Build Wealth by Not Paying Down Your Mortgage

Because I teach professionals and have written on two different, but related, mortgage topics, people are constantly getting them mixed up. These two topics are: 1) how to <u>pay off your mortgage quicker</u> (H.E.A.P.™), and 2) how to <u>never pay off your mortgage</u>, but use your home equity instead to build the most tax-favorable retirement nest egg (Equity Harvesting).

I suppose that's understandable since both H.E.A.P.™ and Equity Harvesting are "Home Equity Management" concepts.

From an advisor's point of view, I have had and continue to receive many phone calls asking me how they can help their clients build **more wealth** using H.E.A.P.™ and in a scenario where clients **DO NOT** pay down debt on their primary residence.

Now that you are a quasi-H.E.A.P.™ expert (since you've nearly finished reading this book), if you were asked how you could build more wealth through H.E.A.P.™ without paying down your mortgage, you would probably scratch your head a little.

Why would anyone use a Home Equity Acceleration Plan and **NOT** pay off a mortgage?

That's what this chapter is going to explain to you—and I think that once you go through it, the light bulb will go on, and you may choose to use H.E.A.P.™ to grow more wealth as described rather than to pay down your mortgage (which is how it is normally used).

SUMMARY OF THE "TRADITIONAL" USE OF H.E.A.P.™

Let's quickly review how H.E.A.P.™ is set up and works. The assumption is that you have a home with debt and some amount of equity and that your goal is to pay off the mortgage as quickly as possible.

1) You first go to your local H.E.A.P.™ advisor and sit down to create a budget for your plan (proper budgeting is a must so you have the most efficient and protective plan)

2) After figuring out your budget, you go to a lender and obtain a Home Equity Line of Credit (HELOC).

3) You access that HELOC in the appropriate amount ($5,000, $10,000, etc.) and use the borrowed funds to pay down the primary mortgage on your residence.

4) You then use the HELOC as your checking account.

5) Remember that when the HELOC is reduced to the point where your next deposit will pay off the entire debt (or more) of the HELOC balance, you need to re-access the HELOC again for the appropriate amount and pay down your primary mortgage again.

What will H.E.A.P.™ accomplish for you?

-It allows you to use "**every available dollar every day**" to pay down mortgage debt.

-The plan works "automatically" to pay down your HELOC since the monthly surplus will be used to pay down that balance every month.

-You live your life as you normally would, and H.E.A.P.™ will help you pay down your primary mortgage quicker than any other plan in the marketplace (with **no $3,500** fee for "magic" software, without a large floating rate primary mortgage, and with the least amount of headaches).

H.E.A.P.™ is a very powerful and simple plan. Why would anyone want to do anything different than this plan?

What if your financial goal is to simply build more wealth vs. the goal of paying off your mortgage quicker?

That's a good question; but, because you read the chapter on Equity Harvesting, you already know some of the basics about how to build "Maximum Wealth with Maximum Security."

If you'll recall, Equity Harvesting is where you remove equity from your home to fund a wealth-building tool where your money will grow tax-free and can be removed tax-free.

Equity Harvesting is certainly one of, if not, the most powerful wealth-building tools we have at our disposal. Having said that, I know for a fact, from talking with hundreds of clients, many simply do not want to incur more debt to build wealth.

Even though the math is crystal clear that Equity Harvesting is a powerful wealth-building tool, many people find it **counter-intuitive** to think that they can build wealth by borrowing money.

Besides being counter-intuitive, many clients don't care if they can build more wealth (even though they should). What they know is that they despise having a mortgage, and it's their life's goal to pay it off as soon as possible (which is why H.E.A.P.™ is the tool of choice for such a person).

HOW TO USE H.E.A.P.™ TO BUILD MORE WEALTH

I'm going to proceed as though you fully understand how H.E.A.P.™ works in its traditional sense and that you understand the basics of why Equity Harvesting can work to build maximum wealth.

What I'm going to explain to you now is the psychology and the math behind how you can use H.E.A.P to build wealth.

Let's work from a few of the assumptions I've alluded to already:

1) Virtually everyone despises their home mortgage and making their monthly payment.

2) People, in general, are not interested in incurring more debt.

3) Equity Harvesting is one of the most powerful wealth-building tools we have at our disposal.

4) Many people do not want to move forward with Equity Harvesting because it requires them to incur more debt (the very thing they loath).

Because of these facts, most people who are introduced to H.E.A.P.™ and Equity Harvesting will mentally gravitate to H.E.A.P.™ because deep down they really want to rid themselves of home mortgage debt.

These same people will very much like the financial outcome of Equity Harvesting; but again, because it requires more debt, from a psychological standpoint they just can't pull the trigger to implement the plan.

COMBINING BOTH H.E.A.P.™ AND EQUITY HARVESTING

Doesn't that title sound odd? How can you combine Equity Harvesting and H.E.A.P.™? It's like mixing oil and water or fire and ice. They just don't go together.

Or do they?

LET'S GO OVER H.E.A.P.™ AS A STAND-ALONE TOOL FIRST

I think the best way to explain to you how you can combine H.E.A.P.™ and Equity Harvesting is to use an example.

Let's use the following assumptions for our client example:

-Husband and Wife (Mr. and Mrs. Smith)

-Ages 45

-2 children

-Home worth = $300,000

-Current debt = $180,000 (has been in place for 5 years)

-Initial mortgage debt = $200,000 (30-year fixed at 6.25%)

-Current mortgage payment = $1,231.43

-Other expenses per month = $2,768.57

- After-tax income per month = $5,000

-Monthly Surplus = $1,000

Mr. and Mrs. Smith have all the options in the world in front of them. They can **implement H.E.A.P.™ in its classic form,** and the outcome as "properly budgeted" would look as follows:

(The client would cycle a $10,000 HELOC with an interest rate of 7%)

How much would Mr. and Mrs. Smith save in total interest as budgeted using H.E.A.P.™?

Months Paid	Months Saved	Years Paid	Years Saved	Interest Paid	Interest Saved
109	191	9.08	15.9	$60,880	$98,715

Not bad, right. The Smiths saved **$98,649** in interest and paid off their home loan in 9.08 years and saved nearly 16 years in mortgage payments.

Are the Smiths happy and ready to move forward with H.E.A.P.™? My guess is they are very happy and are ready to move forward.

NEXT, LET'S GO OVER EQUITY HARVESTING AS A STAND ALONE

Instead of using H.E.A.P.™ to pay off their mortgage, they could remove equity from their home to build maximum wealth. The Smiths have $120,000 of equity in their home. They should be able to remove $60,000 in equity for an Equity Harvesting plan.

There are a few different ways to finance an Equity Harvesting plan; but for simplicity, I'm going to assume the Smiths refinance into a new loan with a balance of $240,000 at 6.25%.

I'm going to assume the new loan has an amortization period of 25 years so the Smiths still pay off their current debt in the same time as the current mortgage. This is not classic Equity Harvesting. In classic Equity Harvesting, the Smiths would obtain an interest-only loan with a 30-year amortization where they would never pay off that debt (but would build maximum wealth elsewhere).

Their new payment for $240,000 worth of debt ($60,000 more than where they started) using a 25-year loan at 6.25% would be $1,583.21. Their current monthly payment is $1,231.43 which is budgeted to have the current remaining debt of $180,000 paid off in 25 years.

The real question for this client is: Would they want to borrow $60,000 to help them grow "Maximum Wealth" if the cost was **$351.78** ($1,583.21-$1,231.43) a month?

Let's run the numbers and see how much wealth the Smiths would build if they borrowed an additional $60,000 from their home to grow in a vehicle where the money will grow tax-free and can be removed tax-free in retirement (cash value life insurance).

If we assumed the money in the EIUL insurance policy grows at a conservative 7.5% a year (the life policy I'm using for this example pegs its growth to the S&P 500 index) from ages 45-65 and then if the Smiths decide to take tax-free income (loans) from the policy in retirement, they could remove **$25,902** every year from ages 70-89 (20 years).

Again, what did that cost the Smiths?

$351.78 every month for 25 years.

What's the comparison for the Smiths if they did not implement an Equity Harvesting plan?

-They would have had an extra $351.78 every month to pay down their mortgage early (H.E.A.P.™), or

-They would have figured out a way to spend/waste the money and not build wealth.

-They could invest the money in stocks and mutual funds.

I'm going to give the Smiths the benefit of the doubt and assume they will invest the $351.78 in the market and that they will earn a 7.5% gross rate of return (same as the life policy).

I will use a 20% blended capital gains/dividend tax rate on the growth in the brokerage account, and I'll assume they put the money into typical mutual funds with a 1.2% annual fee. I'll assume no money management fee. In the industry these assumptions are VERY conservative.

How much could the Smiths remove after-tax from a brokerage account that was funded with $351.78 a month for the 25 years that the mortgage was in place (ages 45-70)?

$14,754 every year from ages 70-89 (20 years)

How much could be removed after-tax from the Equity Harvesting/cash value life insurance policy?

$25,902 every year from ages 70-89 (20 years)

138

This is the power of building wealth through Equity Harvesting. See the following Chart 1 that will show you the difference from what the Smiths could remove from a brokerage account vs. a cash value life insurance policy:

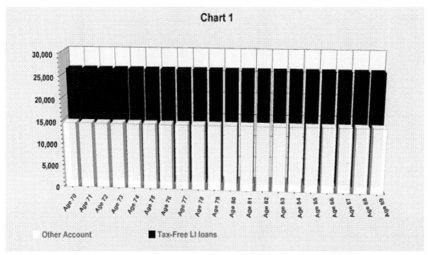

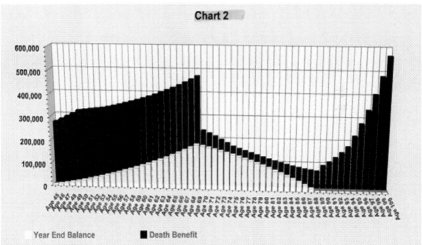

You may be wondering what Chart 2 is?

That's the chart showing how much wealth will pass to the heirs if Mr. Smith dies in any particular year (I assumed the cash value life insurance policy was purchased on Mr. Smith's life).

If he died in year one, the heirs would only receive approximately **$4,230** from the brokerage account.

If he died in year one with an Equity Harvesting plan, the heirs would receive **$270,731**.

The larger set of bars in Chart 2 represents the death benefit which is always substantially higher than what's in the brokerage account.

As you can see, Equity Harvesting is a much better wealth-building tool than H.E.A.P.™.

Actually, with this example, I still budgeted the client to pay off their home mortgage in 25 years (the remaining term of their current mortgage before implementing any kind of plan).

FINALLY, LET ME SHOW YOU HOW TO USE H.E.A.P.™ AS A BIT OF AN IN-BETWEEN PLAN THAT IS PART H.E.A.P.™ AND PART EQUITY HARVESTING

Again, many people who understand Equity Harvesting still will not want to move forward with it for one reason or another (they simply want to rid themselves of debt vs. build maximum wealth being the main reason).

PHSYCOLOGY IS THE KEY

Let me just lay out for you what I know will happen to many people who decide to implement H.E.A.P.™ instead of some form of Equity Harvesting.

Here's the scenario.

Assume you understand Equity Harvesting, but you are nervous about incurring more debt to build wealth (which brings with it more expenses).

Assume you really do like the idea of being debt free and, therefore, choose to move forward with H.E.A.P.™ due to the fact that you can pay off your mortgage in 9.5 years instead of 25 years.

Great. You're happy and the advisor is happy to a point because he/she got you to move from your current do-nothing position.

140

You implement H.E.A.P.™, and you take out a $5,000 HELOC that you are budgeted to pay off in roughly six months. That means you have **$833.33** budgeted surplus every month that will automatically be used to pay down the HELOC.

Let's fast forward six months.

You just received your monthly HELOC account statement and, sure enough, the balance on your HELOC debt is just about zero. Because you are following H.E.A.P.™ in a strict manner, you re-access your HELOC for another $5,000 and send that money to pay down debt on your primary mortgage.

Let's fast forward another six months.

You just received your monthly HELOC account statement and, sure enough, the balance on your HELOC debt is just about zero.

At this time, you have successfully used H.E.A.P.™ for a 12-month period; and to your surprise and delight, it worked. You were able to stay on budget, and you were able to pay down your HELOC every six months.

I want you to assume that, before you access your HELOC for another $5,000, you received a call from your H.E.A.P.™ advisor. He/she wants to sit down with you to do an annual review.

You are happy as a clam with his/her services so far and invite the advisor over to your house the next day.

When the advisor shows up, with him/her are some other wealth-building proposals you have not seen before.

The advisor then sits you down and has a frank discussion about your financial situation. The advisor reiterates that using H.E.A.P.™ in its classic form to pay off debt is certainly better than doing nothing.

However, the advisor is there to show you how to build "Maximum Wealth with Maximum Security" and, as such, starts discussing how H.E.A.P.™ can be used to do so.

The conversation would go something like this:

Advisor: Mr. and Mrs. Smith, I see that you've been able to stay on budget and pay down mortgage debt as we budgeted with H.E.A.P.™

Mr. and Mrs. Smith: Yes. It's been surprisingly easy, and we are very pleased.

Advisor: That's great. So are you comfortable that you'll be able to stay on budget next year and the following years?

Mr. and Mrs. Smith: Oh yes. Actually we are glad you are here. We are going to be making a few more dollars this year, and we'd like you to re-run our H.E.A.P.™ numbers and show us how much more money we'll save on our mortgage interest using the program.

Advisor: I'd be happy to do that, but I wanted to discuss changing how you use H.E.A.P.™ this year and the years beyond.

Mr. and Mrs. Smith: Really. Why would we want to change? We like how it has been working to pay down debt.

Advisor: Yes, I'm sure you do; but my goal for you as your advisor is to show you how to amass the most amount of wealth for retirement while not changing your lifestyle. Would you like me to go over with you what I've brought with me to show you how to build "Maximum Wealth with Maximum Security"?

Mr. and Mrs. Smith: Sure. We'd be happy to see what you have for us.

Advisor: Here's what I'd like you to consider now that you are comfortable that you can, in fact, stay on budget with H.E.A.P.™.

I'd like you to consider taking 50% of the money you have budgeted to pay down your mortgage through H.E.A.P.™ and allocate it to one of the most powerful after-tax/tax-favorable, wealth-building tools available.

This tool is called cash value life insurance; and once funded, the money in the policy **grows tax-free** and **comes out tax-free in retirement**.

The growth in the policy is pegged to the S&P 500 index (minus dividends) and has an annual locking feature so your gains are locked in and are **NOT subject to losses** due to downturns in the stock market.

I have with me an illustration where I assumed you repositioned 50% of the money you normally would allocate to H.E.A.P.™ and instead funded a cash value life insurance policy. I assumed it would grow at 7.5% a year and that you would fund it for 20 years. Then I illustrated that you would remove money from the policy tax-free from ages 66-85 (20 years).

So, in essence, Mr. and Mrs. Smith, I have you allocating $5,000 a year to pay down debt through H.E.A.P.™ and $5,000 to build wealth in a more accelerated manner through the life insurance policy.

As you'll see with the numbers, you would be able to remove **$25,430** income tax-free from your life insurance policy for 20 years starting at age 66.

Mr. and Mrs. Smith, this is a terrific way to build your wealth in a conservative manner; and now that you are comfortable with your budgeting, I believe that this is your best way to accomplish some of your retirement planning goals.

Depending on the psychological mindset of Mr. and Mrs. Smith, their response could be all over the board. Let's look at what the typical responses might be:

1) Well, that looks really impressive; and, while I understand the numbers and the power of what you are telling me, I still really want to pay off my mortgage with H.E.A.P.™ as we've budgeted (even if it doesn't maximize my wealth as much as other plans)

2) Wow. We had no idea you could build that kind of wealth with H.E.A.P.™ and cash value life insurance. We are very interested to learn more.

3) Same as 2) except the clients will ask if they can put all of the money they currently have budgeted into H.E.A.P.™ and instead reposition that money each year into a cash value life insurance policy.

It all depends on the psychology of the client. It's really that simple. Clients who are afraid of debt or are not confident in their ability to budget correctly will stay with H.E.A.P.™ in its traditional platform.

Clients who not only understand the math but also are not fearful of debt or proactively funding wealth-building tools will gravitate to using their money in a more proactive manner as discussed in this chapter and the Equity Harvesting chapter.

H.E.A.P.™ WORKS WITH EQUITY HARVESTING

I wanted to point out one last item of interest. If you happen to read this book or my other book and decide that the best way to build wealth is through never paying off the debt on your home (Equity Harvesting), that doesn't mean that you should not still use H.E.A.P.™

Remember, there is no downside to H.E.A.P.™. If you'll recall from Chapter 4, I illustrated how H.E.A.P.™ would work for someone who spent every dollar they made and didn't have even one dollar of surplus to accelerate the pay down of their mortgage.

The following are the numbers from that example:

-Monthly income (after taxes) = $ 4,252

-First mortgage balance = **$200,000** (house fair market value of $250,000)

-Mortgage monthly payment at 6.25% = $1,231.43

-HELOC interest rate = 6.25%

-New 30-year mortgage

-Total monthly bills (non-mortgage) = $3,020.57

-Total monthly outlay = **$4,252**

144

How much did this Example client save in total interest as budgeted using H.E.A.P.™?

Months Paid	Months Saved	Years Paid	Years Saved	Interest Paid	Interest Saved
342	18	28.50	1.50	$226,267	$17,051

Therefore, even if you choose not to use H.E.A.P.™ in its traditional form to pay down the mortgage quicker because you've chosen to Equity Harvest, you should still use H.E.A.P.™ in an effort to use "**every available dollar every day**" to pay down mortgage debt. Doing so is a risk-free situation for you, and it will ultimately still save you thousands of dollars in mortgage interest.

SUMMARY ON USING H.E.A.P.™ TO BUILD WEALTH

There is nothing wrong with using H.E.A.P.™ in its traditional form. Aggressively paying down mortgage debt by using "**every available dollar every day**" is better than what 99.9% of the American public is doing today.

However, even though I created H.E.A.P.™, to be honest with readers, I do have to state that H.E.A.P.™ is not the best way to grow wealth for retirement.

Equity Harvesting is a much better wealth-building tool. However, many people are not comfortable borrowing money to build wealth.

That's where H.E.A.P.™ in a non-traditional format can come into play. You can create your own hybrid H.E.A.P.™/Equity Harvesting plan by allocating X amount of dollars to aggressively pay down debt through H.E.A.P.™ and Y amount of money to a cash value life insurance policy to grow "Maximum Wealth with Maximum Security."

You can use 50% or 25% or 75% of the money you would normally be budgeting when using H.E.A.P.™. It's up to you and your advisors to figure out the best way to grow your money and still have you feel good about what you are doing.

DO NOT Equity Harvest because you read that you're stupid if you don't build wealth that way.

Believe me, I know there is something to peace of mind; and if you will sleep better at night because you are aggressively paying off debt on your home with H.E.A.P.™, then I recommend you use it in its classic form.

But at the very least, by reading this book and especially if you supplement your reading of this book with <u>The Home Equity Management Guidebook: How to Achieve Maximum Wealth with Maximum Security</u>, you will be armed with the knowledge to make the best decisions for your financial future. (**<u>www.thehomeequtiymanagementguidebook.com</u>**).

Chapter 8
Using a Credit Card
in Conjunction with H.E.A.P.™

As H.E.A.P.™ has become known by more and more people, there are many who are trying to use it in creative ways in an attempt to make it more financially beneficial.

While there is nothing wrong with using H.E.A.P.™ creatively, you need to examine the various uses with a **discerning eye** to make sure it's a truly beneficial way to tweak H.E.A.P.™ .

Using a credit card (Visa, Master Card, American Express, etc.) seems to be one of the more popular variances to H.E.A.P.™ as discussed by some advisors.

I'm going to show you in this brief chapter how to properly use a credit card in conjunction with H.E.A.P.™ and why that may or may not be a good idea.

30-DAY FLOAT

If you buy something today on your credit card, when is your payment actually due?

In other words, when do you have to take money out of your checking account to pay for the item(s) you purchased on the credit card?

This is not a trick question. The answer is that you will need to pay for the item(s) when your credit card bill comes due. The credit card bill is due and payable for most on the same day each month (for the previous month's purchases).

The next question is, "When during your credit card billing cycle did you buy the item?"

Let's look at an example that will lay out exactly how a credit card works when trying to delay payment on new items purchased.

Assume it is January 1 of any given year and that you just opened up and received your new platinum credit card with a $15,000 limit. Further, assume that your billing cycle is set up so that you have to pay any balance on your credit card by the 1st of every month.

Therefore, if you purchased items on your credit card on January 1, the items would have to be paid for on February 1 when your credit card payment is due.

What if you purchased items on January 23rd? Those items would go on your credit card statement and would also be due on February 1 of the following month.

There is a cut-off point somewhere in January where charges after a certain date will be moved to the next month's bill. That date will vary per card but typically is within a few days of the end of your billing cycle.

If I asked if it is true that using a credit card gives you a 30-day float on your bills, is that an accurate statement?

The answer is **yes** for any items purchased on the 1st of the month and **no** for items purchased on any other day thereafter.

HOW MANY 30-DAY FLOATS CAN YOU RECEIVE WITH YOUR CREDIT CARD?

I've heard from dozens of people calling me to inquire about H.E.A.P.™ that they heard the following idea from an advisor pitching mortgage acceleration plans:

"The reason to use a credit card in conjunction with the "new" kind of mortgage acceleration plan is that you can receive a 30-day float every 30 days when using it."

I suppose that sort of makes sense if you say it really fast and don't give it much thought. Sure, every time you cycle bills through a credit card you are delaying payment due on purchases made that month for up to 30 days (although if you buy items periodically throughout the month the float will probably average 15 days).

That sounds great, doesn't it? By using a credit card in conjunction with H.E.A.P.™, you somehow are supercharging the plan by buying yourself a new 30-day float every 30 days.

Does that make any sense now that you've had a second to think about it? It shouldn't.

What's wrong with the idea that, by using a credit card in conjunction with H.E.A.P.™, you receive a "new" 30-day float every 30 days? The answer is that, by using a credit card, you will receive a **one-time,** 30-day float over the **entire life** of the H.E.A.P.™.

Let me just give you an example that should crystallize what I'm trying to explain.

Assume you have $1,800 of non-mortgage expenses throughout the month. Assume you could put all of those expenses on a credit card.

Now let's assume you implement H.E.A.P.™. You obtain a $10,000 HELOC and use that money to pay down debt on your primary/first mortgage.

You then start depositing your paychecks and any other miscellaneous deposits into your HELOC account in an effort to use **"every available dollar every day"** to pay down mortgage debt.

Again, you now have your credit card in hand and will use that to pay your $1,800 worth of bills during the first month.

How is the credit card beneficial? Simple—in the very first month of using H.E.A.P.™, all of the money deposited into your HELOC is used to pay down mortgage debt (which is a good thing).

Further, your HELOC is not accessed the first month to pay bills as you normally would from your checking account because the bills were paid on a credit card where payment is not due for, let's say, 30 days.

Therefore, the credit card was helpful to bump your expenses **one time for 30 days** so the money deposited into your HELOC was used for the entire month to pay down debt.

What about the next month? Do you receive another "new" 30-day float? **NO.**

Once you start using a credit card to pay your bills, you are now in the same 30-day cycle you would have been in had you not used the credit card. Now every month you will use the money deposited into the HELOC to pay bills (except in this case the main bill is the credit card bill that is due at the end of the month).

There is no magic to using a credit card in conjunction with a mortgage acceleration plan. Is it a good idea to use it to obtain the first and only 30-day float? Sure, every little bit helps. Just do not fall prey to the idea that using a credit card somehow buys you a new 30-day float every time you use it. It doesn't.

WHAT IF YOU ALREADY PUT YOUR BILLS ON YOUR CREDIT CARD?

If you already pay your bills on a credit card, then you will not be able to receive even a one-time, 30-day float. And by the way, it's not the end of the world as the 30-day float will have an infinitesimally small effect on the amount of interest saved using H.E.A.P.™

WHY USE A CREDIT CARD IN CONJUNCTION WITH H.E.A.P.™ ?

In the previous paragraph, I stated that using a credit card has a very minor effect on how quickly you will pay off your mortgage.

Then why use one?

I'm sure many of you can guess the answer as you've heard it a number of times before—it's to "earn points."

Points? Sure, points.

I personally use the Sony Card and put all available bills on that credit card. I earn one point for every dollar spent. Then the points can be used/applied towards buying Sony products. When I built a new house a few years ago, I put many of the building supplies on my credit card. I ended up having enough points on my Sony Card to buy a new 41-inch LCD flat screen TV (retail value $3,700 at that time).

My parents have a credit card where they earn Sky Mile points. For every dollar they spend on their credit card, they earn one point. When they earn 25,000 points, they earn a free round-trip airline ticket.

It's funny, but I have many friends who use credit cards for their bills, yet they don't have a card that provides points. I keep telling them that there is no good reason not to use a Sky Mile card or Sony Card or any other "points" card (especially if there is no annual fee). They usually look at me and laugh and ignore my comment.

Think about using a credit card in conjunction with H.E.A.P.™. From our earlier example, I assumed you would put $1,800 worth of bills on the credit card every month. Over 12 months, that equals 21,600 points. That's almost one free round-trip airline ticket or with the Sony Card you could probably buy a new DVD player or Play Station game for the kids.

I also like to use a credit card because it keeps a nice record of what I purchased over the month; and, again, I only have to pay that bill once per month.

AREN'T CREDIT CARDS DANGEROUS?

That's a good question. Many people are afraid of credit cards. Actually, a better statement is that many people are afraid of themselves when they have a credit card in their hands.

I've heard a number of times where people have switched from credit cards to debit cards (where money literally comes out of your checking account when making a purchase) because they did not have the self-discipline to say NO to making purchases.

In other words, the debit card protects people from themselves because, if your checking account goes to zero (or close to it), you won't be able to make new purchases. With a credit card, you may have no money in your personal checking account but $10,000-$20,000 worth of available credit; and you can, in fact, buy items that you don't have the cash to pay for.

I don't want to make demeaning comments in this book about readers, but I will state emphatically that, if you are the kind of person who will run up credit card debt knowing that you will not have the money at the end of the month to pay the bill, YOU ARE NOT a good candidate for H.E.A.P.™

In other words, if you have a history of buying items on your credit cards you can't afford but have mentally decided that it is OK because you can make the "minimum" payment, YOU ARE NOT a good candidate for H.E.A.P.™

Why?

Because with H.E.A.P.™, you are going to obtain a HELOC that may be $10,000 or $25,000 or even larger. You will be able to access that line just as if were a credit card. If you do not have the needed self-discipline to "pay down mortgage debt," you will access that line at times when you can't pay the new debt off; and you will be adding to your overall mortgage debt which is the exact opposite of what you intended to do with H.E.A.P.™.

As stated in Chapter 4 where I explained how and why H.E.A.P.™ works, it should give you "focus" and should not give you free rein to buy items you otherwise can't afford.

When you think about buying "wants" vs. "needs," I hope that you think of the daily interest that will be piling up in your HELOC loan. Hopefully, this will curb, for those who need it, spending habits that have, to date, prevented some from paying down mortgage debt in an accelerated manner.

H.E.A.P.™ is supposed to be a plan that, once budgeted correctly, you can use to pay down mortgage debt as quickly as possible without changing your lifestyle. Having said that, if you lose focus while using H.E.A.P.™, it can work out to your detriment.

CAN YOU USE A CREDIT CARD INSTEAD OF A HELOC TO MAKE H.E.A.P.™ WORK?

I've had this question a number of times as people receive misinformation on how to use a credit card correctly with H.E.A.P.™

The answer is you could use a credit card instead of a HELOC, but it's not a wise choice.

The example would look as follows: Assume instead of obtaining a HELOC you went out and obtained a new credit card (assuming you didn't have one already). Then you put all of your expenses on that credit card and actually paid it off at the end of the month. Then you simply took the extra money ("surplus") from your checking account that you accumulated at the end of the month and applied that towards your primary mortgage (which you can do without H.E.A.P.™).

Isn't that the same thing as using a HELOC when trying to pay down mortgage debt?

No, it's not.

First of all, you are not using "**every available dollar every day**" to pay down mortgage debt. When using a credit card instead of a HELOC, your money is deposited into your normal checking account earning you ZERO interest.

Second, you are creating a lot more work for yourself and are changing the dynamics of how you think about H.E.A.P.™. Sure, anyone can simply send the money left over in their checking account to their primary mortgage company to pay down debt at the end of the month. I imagine everyone reading this book has had that opportunity, and 99% of readers have not done it.

One of the really neat things about H.E.A.P.™ is that, once it is properly budgeted and set up, you can live your life and the **plan will work all by itself**. Your deposits are **automatically** used to pay down maximum debt every day; and at the end of the month, if you have a surplus, it is **automatically** applied to pay down total mortgage debt.

Once you really understand H.E.A.P.™, you'll understand that it's not magic. Besides the ability to use "**every available dollar every day**" to pay down mortgage debt (which is not an insignificant benefit of the plan), the "magical" part of H.E.A.P.™ comes in its simplicity to work for people who literally don't have to do anything after it is set up except live their lives as they normally would.

SUMMARY ON USING CREDIT CARDS IN CONJUNCTION WITH H.E.A.P.™

If you are a good candidate for H.E.A.P.™, you are a good candidate to use a credit card to pay your monthly bills in conjunction with the plan. In general, you are someone with enough self-discipline to refrain from accessing your HELOC to buy "wants" vs. "needs" that you can't pay for at the end of the month.

If that is the case, then you should also have the self-discipline to not buy "wants" vs. "needs" on a credit card used in conjunction with H.E.A.P.™

I would not recommend using a credit card simply to take advantage of the one-time, 30-day float. The benefit will be minimal. However, since you are going to pay your bills at the end of the month through your HELOC and you plan on spending less than you make, using a credit card to obtain "points" is a terrific idea. It will not cost you a dime in interest, and the benefits can be such things as free airline travel, TVs, or gasoline.

H.E.A.P.™ Summary

Would you like to pay off your home mortgage debt 5-10-15+ years early with a plan:

-that does not require you to change your lifestyle;

-that allows you to stay in complete control at all times; and

-that saves the average person with a new loan over $100,000 in mortgage interest?

I asked the above question in the beginning of this book.

Throughout the book I did the best job I could to explain to you:

-how traditional mortgage acceleration plans work (Rounding-Up, Applying the Bonus, and Bi-Weekly Plans);

-how H.E.A.P.™ works to save you thousands of dollars in mortgage interest with a simple plan that won't require you to change your lifestyle (and why it is "**the**" client-friendly mortgage acceleration plan in the marketplace);

-which mortgage acceleration plans to stay away from (the **$3,500** plan and the one that requires you to refinance your entire mortgage into a 1st position HELOC where the interest rate floats monthly);

-why you might want to consider not paying off your home and instead use Equity Harvesting to build wealth; and

-how you can use H.E.A.P.™ to pay off your mortgage and also build wealth in a tax-favorable manner using a hybrid H.E.A.P.™/Equity Harvesting plan.

It is my opinion that there are only two kinds of people in this world:

1) Those who never want to pay off their debt so they can grow "maximum wealth with maximum security" elsewhere; and

2) Those who want to pay off their mortgage debt as soon as possible.

If you fall into category 2), it is my hope that after reading this book you will be armed with the knowledge to determine if H.E.A.P.™ is the right plan to help you rid yourself of mortgage debt as soon as possible with a "no risk" plan.

HOW CAN YOU RECEIVE HELP WITH H.E.A.P.™?

One question you may have after you finish reading this book is how can you use H.E.A.P.™ to pay off your mortgage 5-10-15+ years early saving you tens of thousands of dollars in mortgage interest.

This book will give you plenty of information to understand how H.E.A.P.™ works.

The bad news is that I can't tell you in this book the specifics of how many years you can knock off of your mortgage and how many thousands of dollars in interest you personally could save by using H.E.A.P.™.

If you know a local H.E.A.P.™ advisor, I strongly recommend you contact him/her so he/she can run specific numbers to determine how quickly you can pay off your mortgage and how many tens of thousands of dollars in mortgage interest you will save using the plan.

The good news is that, if you do not know of a local H.E.A.P.™ advisor, you can go to **www.heaplan.com** and fill out a request for information form; and you will be forwarded the contact information of a local advisor who can help you with H.E.A.P.™.

An advisor who is familiar with H.E.A.P.™ and has the needed software to properly budget your plan can usually do so in very short order. You will receive from your local advisor a three-page printout that will tell you specifically how many years H.E.A.P.™ will knock off your mortgage and how many thousands (and for some hundreds of thousands) of dollars in interest you will save.

I can tell you from talking with literally hundreds of interested clients that the anticipation of receiving a H.E.A.P.™ proposal is significant (a bit like waiting for Christmas when you were a kid).

156

I highly recommend that you do not hesitate to fill out the form online to start the process of paying down your mortgage sooner rather than later by using H.E.A.P.™.

AND FINALLY...

Don't forget that **ALL of the profits** from this book will be **donated to local charitable organizations** who will use that money to help fellow citizens who are not financially able to pay their mortgage payments (usually due to a disability, loss of job, or other circumstance outside of their control). You can read more about this charity at **www.HEAPlan.org**.

Please feel free to spread the word about this book to your friends and relatives so they too can learn how to pay off their mortgage debt early and also support a noble charitable cause in the process.

If you would like to get more involved in helping to bring this book to your local church, other local group, Association or Society, please feel free to contact me at info@HEAPlan.com to schedule a phone conference.

Thank you for buying this book, and I hope it helps you in the near and distant future to rid yourself of your home mortgage and other debt.

Roccy DeFrancesco, JD, CWPP™, CAPP™, CMP™
is also the author of:

Bad Advisors: How to Identify Them &
How to Avoid Them
www.badadvisors.com

Retiring Without Risk
www.retiringwithoutrisk.com

The Home Equity Management Guidebook:
How to Achieve Maximum Wealth with Maximum Security
www.thehomeequitymanagementguidebook.com

The Doctor's Wealth Preservation Guide
www.thedoctorswealthpreservationguide.com